Unveiling the Art of Steganography

This book delves into the fundamentals of steganography, the ancient art of hiding messages in plain sight. From the historical roots to modern applications, readers are taken on a journey through the techniques that transform seemingly ordinary content into carriers of covert communication. The book not only demystifies the basics of steganography but also sheds light on its contemporary applications in digital security, forensics, and confidential messaging.

Beginning with the ancient origins of hidden writing, the book builds a clear picture of how steganography has evolved alongside cryptography and cybersecurity. It then moves into the digital realm, explaining with clarity how messages are embedded within images, audio and video files, and how these methods are analyzed, tested, and, ultimately, uncovered.

Balancing theory with application, the text introduces key measures of quality, such as PSNR and MSE, and unpacks practical techniques used for both embedding and detecting hidden data. The discussion of steganalysis tools is especially valuable, giving readers a grounded understanding of the strengths and limitations of current approaches.

Applications are drawn from real-world domains – from digital forensics and cyber defense to secure communications – demonstrating why steganography matters not only as a technical discipline but as a practical skill. The authors also look ahead, surveying the challenges posed by increasingly complex media formats and the potential directions of future research.

Unveiling the Art of Steganography

A Modern Approach

Dr. Urmila Pilania and Dr. Manoj Kumar

CRC Press
Taylor & Francis Group
Boca Raton London New York

CRC Press is an imprint of the
Taylor & Francis Group, an informa business

Designed cover image: Shutterstock ID: 615808274

First edition published 2026
by CRC Press
2385 NW Executive Center Drive, Suite 320, Boca Raton FL 33431

and by CRC Press
4 Park Square, Milton Park, Abingdon, Oxon, OX14 4RN

CRC Press is an imprint of Taylor & Francis Group, LLC

ISBN: 978-1-032-82107-8 (hbk)
ISBN: 978-1-032-82365-2 (pbk)
ISBN: 978-1-003-50413-9 (ebk)

DOI: 10.1201/9781003504139

Typeset in Caslon
by Newgen Publishing UK

Contents

Foreword

Since the beginning of human communication, people have sought clever ways to send messages in secret. From ancient civilizations hiding codes in wax tablets to invisible inks used during wars, the desire to protect information has always been a part of history. In today's digital era, this timeless art has found new life in the form of steganography—a fascinating science that hides information in plain sight within images, audio, videos, or text.

Unveiling the Art of Steganography takes readers on a journey into this hidden world. What makes this book unique is its ability to present a highly technical and specialized subject in a way that is both structured and approachable. The author has skillfully combined the theory behind steganographic techniques with practical insights, real-world applications, and contemporary challenges. This ensures that the book is not just for researchers and academicians, but also for students, practitioners, and curious minds eager to understand how information can be concealed and revealed.

In this book, readers will discover not only the methods of hiding data but also the importance of using such methods responsibly in a world where privacy, security, and ethical concerns are supreme. The text encourages critical thinking about how technology can be both a tool for protection and, if misused, a potential threat.

The strength of this book lies in its clarity, depth, and vision. It does not simply teach steganography as a subject but inspires readers to appreciate it as an evolving art form that continues to adapt to the ever-changing landscape of digital communication.

I am confident that this book will become a valuable companion for anyone interested in the intersections of technology, secrecy, and security. It will guide learners, spark new research ideas, and contribute meaningfully to the field of information security.

I extend my heartfelt congratulations to the author for this significant contribution and invite readers to embark on this enlightening exploration into the art of hidden communication.

Preface

In today's digital age, where information security is of dominant importance, steganography emerges as one of the most fascinating disciplines in the field of data safety. Unlike cryptography, which merely transforms data into an unreadable form, steganography conceals the very presence of the message, thereby ensuring an additional layer of security. This fascinating art and science of hidden communication has evolved over centuries, from ancient practices of secret writing to sophisticated digital methods that seamlessly embed information within images, audio, video, and other multimedia formats.

Unveiling the Art of Steganography is an attempt to present a holistic view of this subject, encompassing both its historical evolution and its modern-day digital applications. The book introduces the fundamental principles, explores classical techniques, and gradually transitions into modern digital approaches that address the complexities of today's cyber-world. Each chapter is structured to balance conceptual clarity with practical illustrations, enabling learners, researchers, and professionals to grasp the subject with ease. Special attention is given to the domain of steganalysis, which complements the study by addressing the detection of hidden information.

This work is not merely a technical exploration but also an invitation to appreciate the creativity and ingenuity behind steganographic techniques. The book also discusses steganalysis—the science of detecting hidden information—thus offering a balanced perspective between concealment and detection.

The intended audience for this book includes undergraduate and postgraduate students of computer science, information-security professionals, forensic investigators, and researchers who are keen to explore the depths of secure communication. By blending history, theory, algorithms, and hands-on tools, this book aims to serve as both a learning resource and a reference guide. This book aims to make the complex world of steganography accessible to all, whether you are an enthusiast intrigued by the art of hidden messages or a professional seeking insights into the nuances of concealing information. The title "Hidden Ink" signifies the concealed narratives that lie beneath the surface, waiting to be unveiled.

I sincerely hope that *Unveiling the Art of Steganography* will inspire readers to look beyond conventional security practices and to explore the hidden layers of digital communication with curiosity, critical thinking, and ethical responsibility.

Acknowledgments

Writing this book, *Unveiling the Art of Steganography*, has been a deeply enriching journey, and I am obliged a responsibility of gratitude to many individuals and my own institution (Manav Rachna University, Faridabad), whose support made it possible.

First and foremost, I express my sincere gratitude to my family for their constant encouragement, patience, and understanding. Their unwavering belief in me has been the foundation on which this work stands.

I would also like to thank my colleagues, mentors, and peers for their valuable guidance, constructive feedback, and inspiring discussions that have shaped my perspective on this subject.

I extend my heartfelt appreciation to my institution, Manav Rachna University, for providing a supportive academic environment, resources, and opportunities that enabled me to carry out my research and transform it into this book.

Finally, I acknowledge the contributions of the broader research community whose pioneering work in steganography and information security has paved the way for this endeavour. Without their collective efforts, this book would not have been possible.

To all who have supported me, directly or indirectly, on this journey—I remain sincerely grateful.

Authors

Dr. Urmila Pilania is an Associate Professor in the Department of Computer Science and Technology, Manav Rachna University, Faridabad, India. Dr. Pilania earned an engineering degree (BTech in computer science and engineering) in 2007 at Guru Jambheshwar University of Science and Technology, Hisar, Haryana, India. She earned an MTech in computer science and technology in 2009 at Vaish College of Engineering, Rohtak, Haryana, India. Dr. Pilania earned a PhD in computer science and technology in 2021 at Manav Rachna University, Faridabad, India. Her primary research interests are in information security, image processing, machine learning, and artificial intelligence.

Dr. Pilania has published many research papers related to information security, object detection, and classification. She is the author of more than 34 research publications with journals and conferences of repute, and some papers are under review or in press with leading publishers. Dr. Pilania has published three national patents, and one design patent is under examination. She has participated in various workshops and faculty development programs. Dr. Pilania has also been associated with many conferences and journals as a reviewer and a member of their technical committee. She has conducted various special sessions at many reputed conferences. Dr. Pilania has delivered guest lectures at some reputed conferences, and she has chaired many sessions at international conferences. Dr. Pilania is currently guiding three PhD research scholars.

Dr. Manoj Kumar is an Associate Professor in the Department of Computer Science and Technology, Manav Rachna University, Faridabad, India. He has more than 14 years' experience, including academics, industry, and research. He earned a PhD in computer vision in 2022 with a thesis titled "Automatic Detection of Moving Object in a Video for Smart Surveillance System". His areas of expertise include computer vision, artificial intelligence (AI), machine learning, image processing, IoT, and blockchain.

Dr. Kumar has published many research papers related to moving object detection and tracking in videos and also extracts features of moving objects or vehicles from video in real-time video surveillance systems. He has published more than 10 papers in SCIE, SCOPUS, and Web of Science indexed journals. Dr. Kumar has presented more than 20 papers at various Scopus-indexed international conferences, and a few have been published as book chapters. He has published four national patents and participated in various workshops and faculty development programs.

Dr. Kumar has been on the reviewer board of the International Conference on Disruptive Technologies (ICDT–2023), the Fourth International Conference on Advancement in Electronics and Communication Engineering (AECE–2023), etc. He has conducted or chaired various special sessions in many reputed conferences and workshops.

Abbreviations

AES	Advanced Encryption Standard
AI	Artificial Intelligence
API	Application Programming Interface
AR	Augmented Reality
ASCII	American Standard Code for Information Interchange
BMP	Bit Map Pixel
BPC	Bit Plain Complexity
B2B	Business to Business
B2C	Business to Consumer
CC	Correlation Coefficient
CNN	Convolution Neural Networks
CPU	Central Processing Unit
CRoSS	Controllable Robust and Secure Image Steganography
CRT	Chinese Remainder Theorem
DB	Decibels
DCT	Discrete Cosine Transform
DES	Data Encryption standards
DFT	Discrete Fourier Transformation
DL	Deep Learning
DWT	Discrete Wavelet Transform
E-Commerce	Electronics Commerce

EOF	End of File
E-payment	Electronics Payment
FOBP	Falling Off Boundary Problem
GAN	Generative Adversial Network
GUI	Graphical User Interface
HTTP	Hypertext Transfer Protocol
IDCT	Inverse Discrete Cosine Transform
IEP	Incorrect Extraction Problem
IWT	Integer Wavelet Transform
JPEG	Joint Photographic Experts Group
KB	Kilo byte
LSB	Least Significant Bit
MAC	Message Authentication Code
MD5	Message Digest Algorithm 5
MPEG	Moving Picture Expert Group
MSB	Most Significant Bit
MSE	Mean Squared Error
MVS	Microsoft Visual studio
NCC	Normalized Correlation coefficient
NPCR	Number of Pixels Change Rate
OTP	One Time Pad
PDF	Portable Document Format
PIM	Permutation Index Modulation
PNG	Portable Network Graphics
PSNR	Peak Signal-to-Noise Ratio
PSO	Particle Swarm Optimization
PVD	Pixel Value Differencing
QDCT	Quantised Discrete Cosine Transform
RGB	Red Green Blue
RMSE	root Mean square Error
ROI	Return on Investment
SNR	Signal-to-Noise Ratio
SQL	structured Query Language
SSIL	Structured Similarity Index Matrix
SSL	Secure Sockets Layer
SVD	Singular Value Decomposition
VR	Virtual Reality
WAN	Wide Area Network
WTO	World Trade Organization

Glossary

Algorithm A step-by-step procedure or set of rules for solving a problem or performing a task, often used in encryption and data hiding.

Authentication The process of verifying the identity of a user or system before granting access to information.

Bit The smallest unit of digital data, representing either 0 or 1.

Cryptography The science of securing communication through encryption and decryption techniques.

Cipher An algorithm used for encrypting or decrypting data.

Cover Medium The original digital file (such as an image, audio, or video) used to hide secret data in steganography.

Data Hiding The process of embedding secret information within digital media without significantly altering its appearance or quality.

Decryption The process of converting encrypted or hidden data back into its original, readable form.

Digital Watermarking Embedding a visible or invisible mark within digital media to prove ownership or authenticity.

Discrete Cosine Transform (DCT) A mathematical technique used to transform signals or images into frequency components, often applied in JPEG compression and steganography.

Discrete Wavelet Transform (DWT) A signal processing technique used for data compression and steganography in the frequency domain.

Encryption The process of converting plain information into unreadable text to prevent unauthorized access.

Hash Function A mathematical function that converts data into a fixed-size string of characters, commonly used for integrity verification.

Information Hiding A broader concept that includes steganography, watermarking, and cryptography to secure or conceal data.

Key A piece of information used in encryption, decryption, or embedding/extraction of hidden data.

Least Significant Bit (LSB) The smallest bit in a byte, commonly used in image steganography to embed secret data without visibly altering the image.

Payload The secret message or data embedded within a cover medium.

Plaintext The original, readable form of information before encryption or hiding.

Pseudorandom Number Generator (PRNG) An algorithm that generates sequences of numbers that mimic randomness, often used in security applications.

Robustness The ability of a steganographic system to resist attacks, distortions, or modifications while still retaining hidden data.

Steganalysis The science of detecting and analyzing hidden data within digital media.

Steganography The art and science of hiding secret information within ordinary digital files so that its existence is concealed.

Watermark A hidden pattern or signal embedded into media, primarily for copyright protection and authentication.

Keywords

A
Adaptability
Adaptive pixel modification
Analytical Attack
Anti-steganography
Attacks
Attacks Detection
Audio
Augmented Reality
Authentication
Authorisation

B
Baboon
Bit Positioning
Bit-Plane Complexity
Blockchain Integration
Brute Force Attack

C
Cryptography
Cover file
Carrier
Concealing algorithm
Ciphertext
Copyright protection
Cryptanalysis
Cryptographic key
Credit card
Copyright security
Cover multimedia file
Concealing process
Cropping attack
Computation overhead analysis
Convolutional neural networks
Countermeasures

D
Digital forensics
Decryption

Digital watermarks
Distorted audio
Digital media
Digital signatures
Digital wallet
Debit card
Digital images
Deep learning
Discrete cosine transform
Digital multimedia
Discrete wavelet transform
Digital watermarking techniques
Deepsteg
Digital invisible ink
Deep fake

E
Extraction algorithm
Encryption
Embedding capacity
Efficiency
E-commerce
E-payment
E-wallet
Encoding
Embedding
Extraction process
Entropy

F
Fraud detection
Fingerprinting
Future trends in steganography

G
Global Business

H
Historical
Hidden data
Hidden secret data
Hide information
Hidden information
Histogram

I
Information security
information
Information encryption
Information embedding
Imperceptibility
Image processing
Internet
Internet banking
Image steganography
Invertible steganography network
Integrity
Information exchange
Integer wavelet transforms
Information encryption

J
JPEGsnoop Tool
JPEG Images
JPEG compression

K
KNN

L
Least Significant Bit
Lena

M
Malicious tasks
Mean square error
Merchants
Micropayment
Microsoft visual studio
Multimedia security
Multimodal steganography

N
Network Watermarking
Network security

O
OpenStego Analyzer
OpenPuff
OpenCV

P
Payload
PDF
Peak Signal to Noise
Peppers
Perceptibility
Permutation Index Modulation
Pixel
Pixel Value Differencing
Plaintext
Protect data
PSNR

Q
Quality of Cover
Quantized Discrete Cosine Transform
Quantum Computing
Quantum Watermarking

R
Reliability
Retrieval Process
Retrieved JPG Secret Image
Retrieved Secret Data
Retrieved Secret Image
Reverse Watermarking
Robustness

S
Steganography process
Secret information
Secret message
Secret writing
Security
Singular value decomposition
Spatial domain steganography
Steganalysis
Steganalysis tools
Steganography
Stegdetect
Stegexpose
Stego file
Stego frame
Stego key
Stego visual quality
Stegsecret
Substitution
Symmetric encryption

T
Transform

V
Video
Video steganography
Viola-jones algorithm
Virtual reality
Visual quality

W
Watermarking
World Trade Organization

X
X-Box

1

Introduction to Ancient Roots of Steganography

1.1 Introduction

In digital communication, secret information transmission faces many issues that requires more attention. The security of information during communication plays a vital role in this era of the digital world. There are many ways through which secret information can be protected across the channel during transmission. The encryption process only scramble the secret message, but its existence is known to everyone. If we can use an advanced technique that can hide the existence of a secret message, then security can be improved. Steganography is hiding a secret message inside a cover file, which can protect unauthorized access. It is originated from Greek roots (στεγαν′ος, γραφ-ειν), which means "hidden writing" [1].

The main objective of steganography is not only to deliver the secret message, but also to hide the existence of the secret message. No one other than the sender and receiver can detect whether a secret message exists. In case if message existence is known to anyone on the web other than sender and receiver then propose of steganography dilutes. Steganography may use any cover file such as text, image, audio, video, and communication protocols [2].

These days, image and video steganography are very popular among researchers and academicians. Images are the most widely used multimedia files on the web for transmitting data from one source to another. Video steganography is gaining popularity because of its large size and dynamic nature. Steganography tools are also available, which could be utilized to embed the secret message in any multimedia file. These tools can be installed on a device or run online to embed the hidden

DOI: 10.1201/9781003504139-1

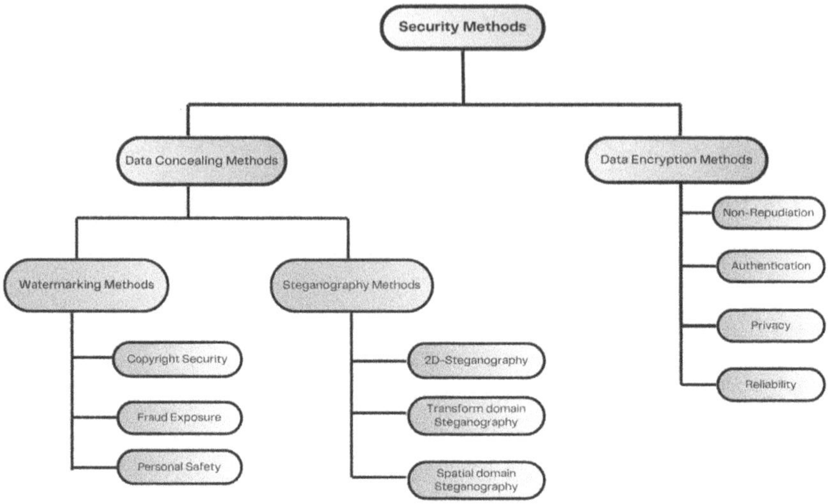

Figure 1.1 Information security methods [5].

data. Steganalysis techniques and tools exist to retrieve the secret message. Steganalysis is the process of retrieving the secret message from the cover file. Steganalysis can also be performed in both the spatial and transform domains. The various information security methods are presented [3] in Figure 1.1 along with their sub-categories.

1.2 Steganography

It is the process of hiding a secret message in any cover file so that a third party is not aware of the existence of the secret message. Hiding secret messages is not new among researchers and academicians, but it has existed for the past 2,000 years. It was used traditionally in ancient times, but it has taken a digital form these days. Traditional steganography is also known as physical steganography. This means that some physical medium is required to hide the secret message. Sovereigns in ancient Greece usually select the messengers to transfer the secret message [4].

They used to shave their heads, write a secret message, and wait for the hair to grow again. After proper hair growth, they sent a messenger to the receiving party. They again shave off the hair at the receiver's side and retrieve the secret message. At that time, the Chinese used fine silk to embed the hidden message. Silk pieces were ground into small pellets. The messenger swallowed these small pellets, and these messengers were sent to the receiver, where they retrieved the secret message.

After physical steganography, another method was utilized to embed the secret message, and that method was known as ordinary-object steganography. In 1914, invisible ink was used to write the secret message on the paper, and the secret message written was invisible to a third party. A hidden secret message was retrieved at the receiver end using a liquid like juice, milk, or vinegar. After applying these liquids to the paper, the secret message became visible to the receiver when it was heated. In this modern era of the digital world, another type of steganography, known as digital steganography, is used to embed the secret message. Digital steganography includes digital cover files like text, images, audio, video, etc. [6].

1.2.1 Steganography Process

To understand the steganography process, it is essential to know about some of the terminologies that are part of it. The digital steganography process is shown in Figure 1.2 [7, 8]:

- **Carrier:** Digital file may have any form, including text, image, audio, and video. It is used to hide the secret message.
- **Secret Message:** The information may be in text, image, audio, or video, which the sender transmits to the recipient. Its

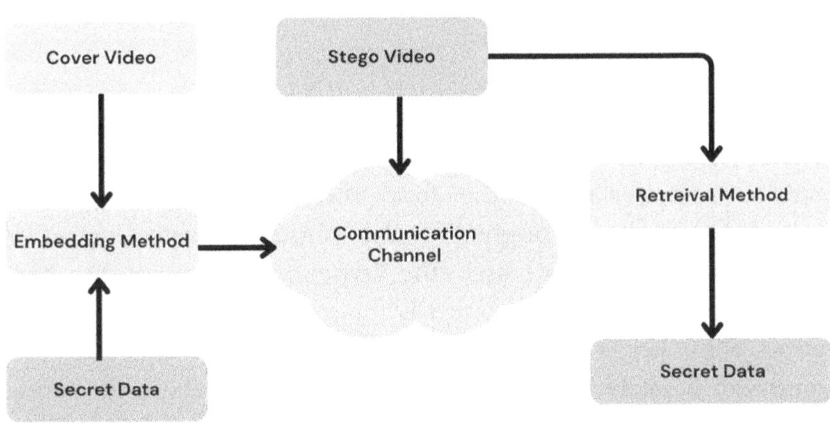

Figure 1.2 Steganography process.

existence is not known to the third party except the sender and receiver.

- **Stego Key:** This key is used to govern the embedding of secret information in the cover file, and at the receiver's end, it is again used to retrieve the hidden information from the cover file. It is optional; the user may use the key to improve the security.
- **Concealing Algorithm:** The algorithm that is used to embed the secret message in the cover file. After embedding a message in a cover, the new file, known as the stego file, carries the hidden message.
- **Extraction Algorithm:** The algorithm used to retrieve the secret message from the stego file was created one step before. It is the reverse process that is carried out during the embedding of a hidden message.

Steganography is further divided depending on the type of cover file used.

1.2.2 Cryptography vs Watermarking vs Steganography

Cryptography and watermarking are sometimes used interchangeably with steganography, but all three terms are very different. The security system mainly has two forms: information encryption and information hiding. Under information encryption, cryptography comes into play, and information hiding includes watermarking and steganography. These three terms are discussed in Table 1.1 in detail based on various parameters [9].

1.2.2.1 Cryptography "Crypt-" stands for "concealed" and "graphy" means "writing". It is the process in which a user converts the source secret information into another form, and at the recipient end, it is again decoded into the original form. It is tough to detect the coded data by an unauthorized user. The cryptography process has been presented in Figure 1.3. Plaintext is the information that the sender carries. Some key is applied to the plaintext, and then converted into ciphertext. Ciphertext is the encoded form of plaintext information. A key is required to convert plaintext into ciphertext, and again at the receiver side, the same or a different key is used to decrypt the

Table 1.1 Information Encryption vs Information Embedding [14, 15]

	INFORMATION ENCRYPTION	INFORMATION EMBEDDING	
PARAMETERS	CRYPTOGRAPHY	WATERMARKING	STEGANOGRAPHY
Description	Secret writing	Information embedding	Information embedding
Secret Data	Unreadable, scrambled information	Information may or may not be visible	Information is hidden
Aim	Not understandable	Copyright information	Hide the existence of information
Cover	Text	Images most of the time	Any multimedia file
Perceptibility	Always visible	Sometime visible	Secret information is hidden
Attacks	Cryptanalysis	Image-processing attacks	Steganalysis, image-processing attacks
Key	Public and private key	Not compulsory	Not compulsory
Security	Less secure	Secure	High security
Issues	Managing key	Robustness	Imperceptibility, embedding capacity, robustness
Output	Plain/Ciphertext	Images in many cases	Text, image, video

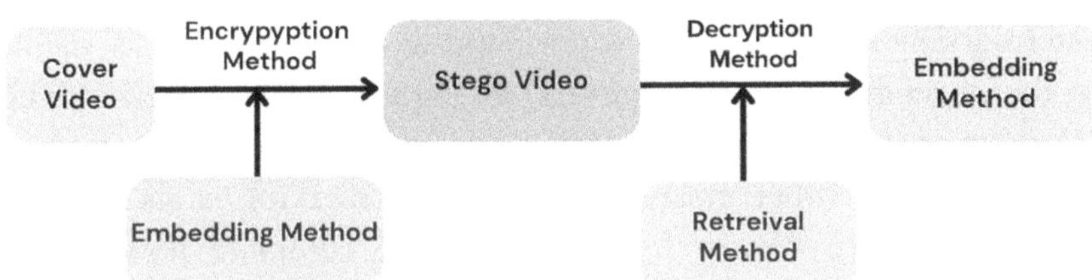

Figure 1.3 Cryptography process [10].

message. Encryption is of two types: one that uses the same key on both the sender and receiver sides, which is known as symmetric-key encryption. If different keys are used for encryption and decryption of a message, that is known as asymmetric-key encryption.

Cryptanalysis techniques are used to break the ciphertext. By using these techniques, the robustness of the cryptography could be measured. If it is hard to break the ciphertext, a more robust and reliable cryptography technique will be needed. The main attributes of the cryptography techniques include: confidentiality, authenticity, integrity, and non-repudiation [11]. Confidentiality means only the source and destination know the key and can access the information. A cryptography algorithm confirms the authenticity of the secret information, so only the sender and receiver can access the hidden message.

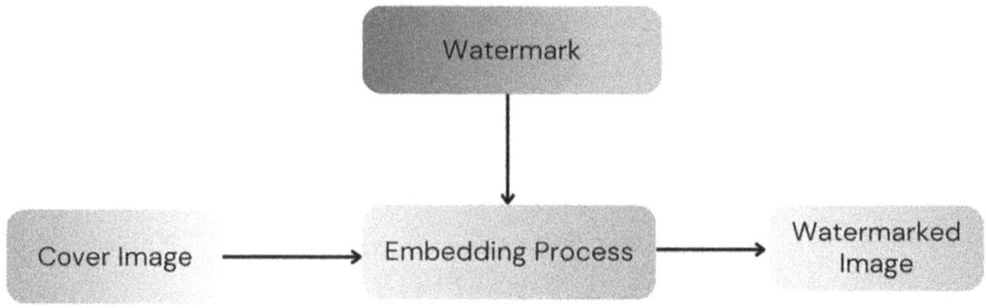

Figure 1.4 Watermarking process.

Integrity confirms the non-editing of the secret message during transmission. Non-repudiation property authorizes the source person from whom the secret message originates.

1.2.2.2 Watermarking Digital watermarks exist in many forms, like text, image, and logo. It delivers the guarantee of its authenticity. Watermarking is further classified into visible and invisible watermarking [12]. In visible watermarking, the watermark is visible on the cover file as an image, text, or logo. Invisible watermarking is hidden in the background of a logo, image, or text, but is identifiable by some other means. Invisible watermarking is also known as steganography. Figure 1.4 represents the complete flow of the watermarking process [13]. The primary purpose of watermarking is to provide copyright protection, fraud detection, personal security, and practical data storage.

1.2.2.3 Steganography Steganography is the science of embedding secret data within a cover file. The third party must not be aware of the existence of the hidden secret data. The hidden secret data could be forwarded to the destination, and the recipient stores it. If anyone detects hidden data, then the objective of steganography fails. Steganography and cryptography can be merged to improve the robustness of the hidden data. To check the reliability and robustness, many steganalysis techniques also exist. Steganalysis techniques can detect hidden data. These techniques include translation, clipping, rotation, compression, geometric correction, gamma correction, and many more.

1.2.3 Types of Steganography

Figure 1.5 represents different types of steganography techniques. These techniques include four types, which are explained in brief as follows:

In information-retrieval techniques, users check whether the carrier file is recovered after extracting the secret message from it. These techniques are further divided into reversible and irreversible techniques. The stego file is dissolved into the original and hidden messages using reversible techniques. However, in the case of irreversible techniques, it is not necessary to generate both the original and secret messages [16]. The next type of technique mentioned is 2D and 3D steganography.

3D steganography is getting attention because of its length, breadth, and height. 3D files have a large number of options for embedding the secret message. The next type of steganography is categorized into spatial and transform domains. The spatial domain is simple, and we must overwrite the pixel's value. However, the transform domain is complex as it embeds data in the frequency domain, providing more robustness to the proposed method. Based on the type of carrier file, steganography is divided into text, image, audio, and video steganography techniques.

Table 1.2 completely compares text, audio, image, and video steganography techniques. Image steganography and video

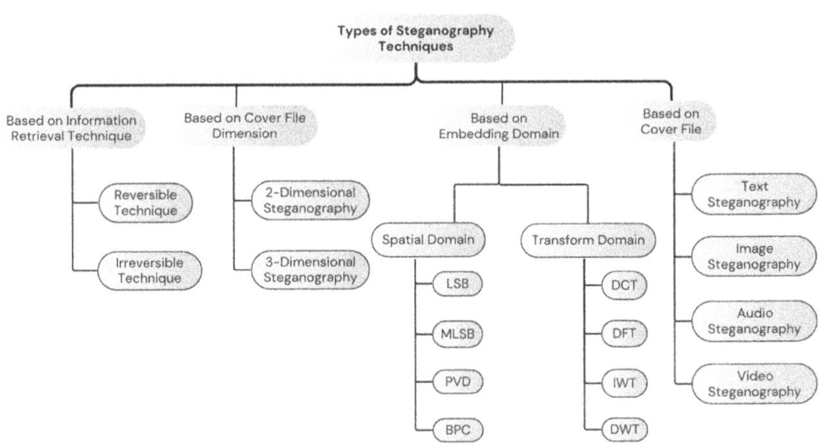

Figure 1.5 Types of steganography techniques.

Table 1.2 Steganography Techniques Based on Carrier File [17]

PARAMETER	TEXT STEGANOGRAPHY	AUDIO STEGANOGRAPHY	IMAGE STEGANOGRAPHY	VIDEO STEGANOGRAPHY
Carrier	Text	Audio	Image	Video
Secret Message	Text	Text, images, and audio	Text, images	Any type
Efficiency	Low	More than text	Efficient	Highly efficient
Speed	Speed varies	Speed is low because it works with models and selects only one model at a time.	Fastest	Low speed, as the video is divided into frames, embedding takes place.
Concealing Capacity	It only conceals text with very low capacity	It can only hide bits of secret data	Higher than audio steganography	More than one image or audio sample can be used to conceal secret data
Robust	Easily detectable	More robust	The cover file size should be large enough to embed secret data properly	More flexible and more robust
Security	No padding around secret data, so it's less secure	More secure due to the large size of the cover file	The size of the data embedded affects the security of the technique	More secure due to flexibility
Stego Visual Quality	Poor	Distorted audio	The quality of the stego is fine, but there are chances of detection of the secret data.	Good quality stego image and less chances for detection of secret data

steganography are more popular. Images are the most commonly used medium of communication on the web. Video files are flexible due to their large size and dynamic nature, so less chance of detection of secret data in video steganography. As shown in the table, many characteristics are chosen to differentiate these techniques, including security, robustness, embedding capacity, speed, cover file used, and many more.

1.2.4 Measures of Steganography

The outcome of the steganography techniques is measured through parameters such as embedding capacity, robustness against attacks, imperceptibility, etc. [18]. Embedding capacity is the amount of information that can be concealed in the cover file without affecting its visual quality. Embedding capacity is measured in kilobytes (KB). Image-processing attacks test the robustness of the steganography techniques.

Robustness is the ability of the stego file to remain unaffected when different attacks are applied. Imperceptibility compare the quality of the stego file with the original cover file. Imperceptibility can be measured using parameters like Peak Signal-to-Noise Ratio (PSNR), Mean Squared Error (MSE), Structural Similarity Index Matrix (SSIM), histogram analysis, etc. A histogram measures frequency distribution in the stego and the cover file. Entropy could also be used to check the randomness of the stego and original cover files.

1.2.5 Application of Steganography

These days, digital steganography has applications in various fields like the military, medical data, business, online transactions, banking, biometrics, printing, social sites, and many more, as shown in Figure 1.6. Steganography has already made an atmosphere of supportive observance, which has produced numerous valuable applications. In steganography, embedded secret data is unknown to anyone, so it

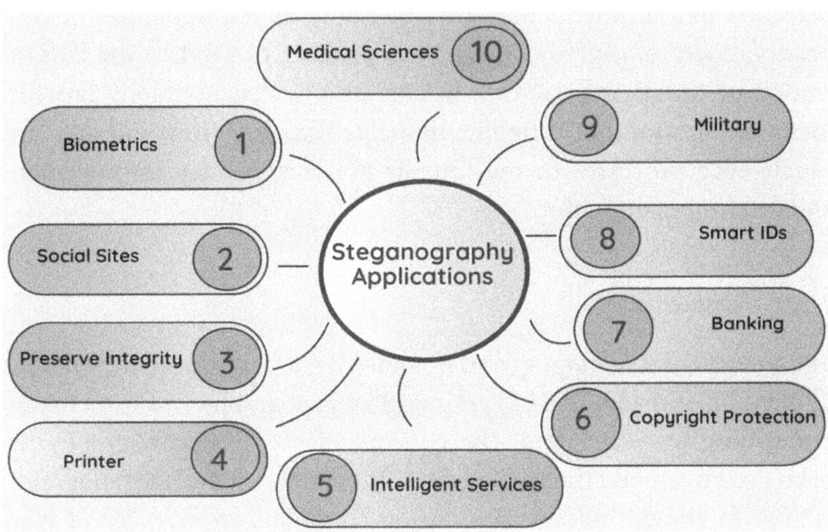

Figure 1.6 Applications of steganography [20].

maintains the hidden data's integrity, authentication, and validation. Integrity means no updation in the original secret data. It also validates that the information comes from the right person [19].

The source and destination are also authorized to send and receive the secret data. Digital media is promoting steganography as everyone uses the web to transmit data. Users use social sites and email accounts for transmission. The primary concern among the researchers and academicians is the security of the secret data.

Steganography has been used several times in military and intelligence operations to transmit secret data. It has often been employed in digital watermarking to conceal copyright data in multimedia files. Copyright helps recognize the data's owner and prevents the document's illegal use or spreading. Steganography also allows concealed communication in situations where encryption may draw suspicion. It does not attract the attention of the third parties because of its hidden nature. It also plays a vital role in digital foreign policy. Ethical hackers use steganalysis techniques to analyze a stego file to find the hidden secret data, which in turn could help find the actual criminal.

Intellectual property rights can be saved by concealing secret data in the cover file. It saves unauthorized users from illegal use of data on the web. Steganography can be used for authentication and tamper detection in multimedia files. By concealing digital signatures or verification codes in digital content, it is possible to validate the authorization of the digital content. In conclusion, steganography provides many applications in different domains, ranging from military and intelligence processes to multimedia content, privacy improvement, and forensic examination.

1.2.6 Motivation

The concept of steganography is not new; it was introduced by Johannes Trithemius in 1449. In 1449, physical steganography was used for the embedding of secret data. The concept of object steganography has been used to embed the hidden data. These days, digital steganography is used to embed hidden data during communication. A lot of work has already been done on digital steganography. Digital steganography includes text, image, audio, video, and protocols as the cover files.

Image steganography has been the focus of several research scholars. But video steganography is also very popular these days due to its large size and dynamic nature. However, a number of issues still exist with the steganography techniques. Some of the problems are listed as follows [21, 7, 22]:

- Low embedding capacity
- The poor visual quality
- Less robust against image processing attacks
- Integrity of secret data
- Change in the format of the cover
- Change in the format of secret data
- High computational cost
- Large embedding time
- Ample extraction time, etc.

Many researchers are already working on these issues, but no one can fix all the issues altogether. Individuals can fix one or two issues, which is also evident from the literature. As all these problems depend on one another, enhancing one problem results in other issues.

1.2.7 Conclusion

In conclusion, this chapter presents a survey of steganography, a process used to conceal secret data within a cover file, known only to the sender and receiver. Steganography has a rich history, evolving from physical to object and, ultimately, digital forms. Digital steganography encompasses various media such as text, images, audio, and video, each classified based on the type of cover file used. This chapter also introduces the basic concepts of steganography, cryptography, and watermarking, shedding light on their interconnections. Furthermore, it explains measures of steganography and the factors that drive its acceptance. Additionally, the chapter provides modern applications of steganography, showcasing its relevance in contemporary contexts.

1.2.8 Summary

Chapter 1 explores the fundamentals of steganography techniques. It begins by briefly discussing the basics of steganography. Within

Section 1.1, the categorization of security systems into two main techniques: data concealing and data encryption has been provided. Data-concealing techniques are further categorized into watermarking and steganography. The chapter explains the cryptography, watermarking, and steganography processes in subsequent subsections. Steganography is further elaborated upon in the following subsection, where it is categorized into four possible types. The primary emphasis of this chapter is on steganography based on cover files, which is thoroughly explored. These types are described in tabular format to aid comprehension, enabling a clearer understanding of the concepts. The effectiveness of steganography is depends on various parameters, which are briefly explained. Finally, this chapter concludes by providing insights into the practical applications of steganography, offering a comprehensive overview of its utility.

References

[1] Kour, J., & Verma, D. (2014). Steganography techniques: A review paper. *International Journal of Emerging Research in Management & Technology*, *3*(5), ISSN, 2278–9359.

[2] Pilania, U., Kumar, M., & Mittal, V. (2023). Performance evaluation of LSB steganography based on multiple image formats. *Journal of Discrete Mathematical Sciences and Cryptography*, *26*(7), 1911–1924.

[3] Hu, K., Wang, M., Ma, X., Chen, J., Wang, X., & Wang, X. (2024). Learning-based image steganography and watermarking: A survey. *Expert Systems with Applications*, *249*, 123715.

[4] Cox, I. J., Miller, M. L., Linnartz, J. P. M., & Kalker, T. (2018). A review of watermarking principles and practices. In K. K. Parhi and T. Nishitani (eds), *Digital signal Processing for Multimedia Systems* (pp. 461–485). Marcell Dekker Inc.

[5] Desmedt, Y. (1987, August). Society and group-oriented cryptography: A new concept. In *Conference on the Theory and Application of Cryptographic Techniques* (pp. 120–127). Springer Berlin Heidelberg.

[6] Pilania, U., Tanwar, R., & Nandal, N. (2022). Exploring face detection and recognition in steganography. In U. Pilania, R. Tanwar, and N. Nandal (eds), *Unleashing the Art of Digital Forensics* (pp. 181–214). CRC Press.

[7] Pilania, U., Tanwar, R., & Kaushik, K. (2022, June). Steganography tools and their analysis concerning distortion in stego image. In *International Conference on Advances in Data Science and Computing Technologies* (pp. 531–538). Springer Nature Singapore.

[8] Hamid, N., Yahya, A., Ahmad, R. B., & Al-Qershi, O. M. (2012). Image steganography techniques: An overview. *International Journal of Computer Science and Security)*, *6*(3), 168–187.
[9] Johnson, N. F., & Jajodia, S. (1998). Exploring steganography: Seeing the unseen. *Computer*, *31*(2), 26–34.
[10] Provos, N., & Honeyman, P. (2003). Hide and seek: An introduction to steganography. *IEEE Security & Privacy*, *1*(3), 32–44.
[11] Cheddad, A., Condell, J., Curran, K., & Mc Kevitt, P. (2010). Digital image steganography: Survey and analysis of current methods. *Signal Processing*, *90*(3), 727–752.
[12] Majeed, M. A., Sulaiman, R., Shukur, Z., & Hasan, M. K. (2021). A review of text steganography techniques. *Mathematics*, *9*(21), 2829.
[13] Judge, J. C. (2001). *Steganography: past, present, future* (No. UCRL-ID-151879). Lawrence Livermore National Lab. (LLNL), Livermore, CA (United States).
[14] Cox, I., Miller, M., Bloom, J., Fridrich, J., & Kalker, T. (2007). *Digital watermarking and steganography*. Morgan kaufmann.
[15] Kunhoth, J., Subramanian, N., Al-Maadeed, S., & Bouridane, A. (2023). Video steganography: Recent advances and challenges. *Multimedia Tools and Applications*, *82*(27), 41943–41985.
[16] Mstafa, R. J., & Elleithy, K. M. (2017). Compressed and raw video steganography techniques: A comprehensive survey and analysis. *Multimedia Tools and Applications*, *76*, 21749–21786.
[17] Hanafy, A. A., Salama, G. I., & Mohasseb, Y. Z. (2008, November). A secure covert communication model based on video steganography. In *MILCOM 2008-2008 IEEE Military Communications Conference* (pp. 1–6). IEEE.
[18] Lee, S. J., & Jung, S. H. (2001, June). A survey of watermarking techniques applied to multimedia. In *ISIE 2001. 2001 IEEE International Symposium on Industrial Electronics Proceedings (Cat. No. 01TH8570)* (Vol. 1, pp. 272–277). IEEE.
[19] Potdar, V. M., Han, S., & Chang, E. (2005, August). A survey of digital image watermarking techniques. In *INDIN'05. 2005 3rd IEEE International Conference on Industrial Informatics* (pp. 709–716). IEEE.
[20] Prabhakaran, N., & Shanthi, D. (2012). A new cryptic steganographic approach using video steganography. *International Journal of Computer Applications*, *49*(7), 32–42.
[21] Eggers, J. J., Baeuml, R., & Girod, B. (2002, April). Communications approach to image steganography. In *Security and Watermarking of Multimedia Contents IV* (Vol. *4675*, pp. 26–37). SPIE.
[22] Pilania, U., Tanwar, R., & Gupta, P. (2021). Performance analysis of open-source image steganography tools. *Journal of Engineering and Applied Sciences*, *8*(1), 50–67.

2

Symmetric Encryption and XOR-Based Model for E-Commerce Ecosystem

2.1 Introduction

Electronic commerce (e-commerce) is still relatively unfamiliar to many Indians. Generally, e-commerce transactions are more commonly used by the upper-middle-class segment of society. There is no universally accepted definition of e-commerce, although it broadly refers to transactions conducted electronically. The term "e-commerce" is derived from two English words: "E," which stands for "electronic," and "Commerce," which refers to trade or commercial activities. Etymologically, "electronic" relates to the science of electricity, electronic devices, or anything associated with electronics and technology, while "commerce" refers to the exchange of goods and services [1].

In practical terms, e-commerce refers to trade transactions via electronic media, typically through internet-connected systems. From a terminological standpoint, the World Trade Organization (WTO) defines e-commerce as encompassing all activities related to producing, distributing, marketing, selling, and delivering goods or services conducted electronically. Similarly, the Alliance for Global Business defines e-commerce as any value-based transaction that involves transferring information, products, services, or payments over electronic networks. Through these digital platforms, goods and services of economic value are designed, produced, promoted, listed in catalogs, stored in inventories, purchased, and delivered. E-commerce can be understood from four key perspectives [2, 3]:

DOI: 10.1201/9781003504139-2

- E-commerce delivers goods, services, information, and payments through computers or electronic devices.
- From this viewpoint, e-commerce uses technology to automate business transactions and workflows, enhancing operational efficiency.
- E-commerce serves as a tool to meet the needs of companies, management, and consumers by reducing service costs, improving product quality, and accelerating the delivery of goods and services.
- In this context, e-commerce enables the buying and selling goods, products, and information through the internet and other digital channels.
- A more detailed definition describes e-commerce as an electronic business model that emphasizes transactions between individuals using the internet to exchange goods or services, either between two organizations (B2B) or between businesses and individual consumers (B2C).

2.1.1 Transaction Payment System E-Commerce (E-Payment)

A payment system is a framework of procedures and regulatory instruments that enables institutions to facilitate transactions between parties making and receiving payments. Within this system, banking institutions play a crucial intermediary role, acting as facilitators that connect payers and recipients in transferring funds. From a legal standpoint, banks are authorized entities that can directly enable and execute fund transfers between parties.

Today, payment systems have evolved beyond national boundaries and now operate globally. Payment is not an isolated or spontaneous process but a fundamental outcome of economic transactions. Payments can range from simple, traditional methods that do not involve banks to complex transactions that require the involvement of financial intermediaries to ensure security and efficiency [4].

E-payments are a modern form of payment conducted via the internet, allowing customers to pay for goods and services online. E-payments rely on the digital data to store, process, and transfer money, serving as a substitute for physical cash in the online marketplace—a core component of the e-commerce paradigm. The implementation of E-payment systems typically involves several key participants [5, 6]:

- Issuers: Banks or non-bank financial institutions that issue the electronic payment instruments used in online transactions.
- Customers (Consumers): Individuals who pay online for goods or services.
- Merchants (Sellers): Businesses or individuals that accept electronic payments for products or services sold online.
- Regulators: Typically, government bodies that establish and enforce the legal framework governing electronic payment systems.
- Acquirers: Financial institutions that manage merchant accounts and handle the authorization and processing of payment card transactions, including transmitting cardholder payment instructions.

2.1.2 Benefits of E-Payment

Using e-payment facilities provides numerous benefits for both sellers and buyers, including [7, 8]:

- Universal Transactions: The transaction system is simple and can be carried out universally, as long as it remains within the country's jurisdiction.
- Enhanced Security: E-payment systems offer better security than cash transactions or personal account transfers, reducing the risk of theft or fraud.
- Time and Energy Efficiency: Payments can be made online, streamlining the process and significantly saving time and effort for both parties.
- Flexibility: Since the system operates online, e-payments can be made anytime and anywhere, offering greater convenience and accessibility.

2.1.3 Types of E-Payment

Micropayment: It is a form of electronic payment designed for small-value transactions conducted over the internet or other digital platforms. They are commonly used due to their practicality and convenience, especially for frequent and low-value payments. Benefits of micropayments include [9, 10]:

- Practical and flexible transactions without the need for physical cash.
- Mobility – transactions can be completed from anywhere using a mobile device.
- Time-efficient processing.
- Versatility – functional for various types of bill payments such as telephone, internet, electricity, and banking services.
- Standard micropayment methods include mobile payment, mobile parking, mobile ticketing, and mobile banking.

E-Wallet: It is a digital alternative to traditional payment systems, enabling users to make secure online transactions without revealing financial details. Registered users can send or receive money using an email address or a mobile number, offering convenience and safety.

Credit Card: It enables users to make purchases on credit, with the issuer lending money for the transaction. Smart cards, a credit card embedded with a computer chip, offer greater data storage and multi-functionality. Depending on the chip's features, these cards can be used for calls, e-payments, and other services.

Debit Card: It is issued by a bank and directly linked to a customer's savings account. It allows electronic payments by deducting funds directly from the user's bank balance.

Cash on Delivery (COD): This is a payment method through which the buyer pays in cash upon receiving the goods. While it bypasses the full convenience of online transactions, it offers added security for the buyer by ensuring the product is delivered and verified before payment is made.

2.1.4 Cryptography

Cryptography originates from the Greek words *crypto*, meaning "secret", and *graphia*, meaning "writing". In modern terms, cryptography refers to encrypting data—transforming readable information into an unreadable format using an encryption key. Only individuals with the correct decryption key can access the original data. Cryptography plays a vital role in everyday applications, including: ATM transactions, online banking, mobile banking, and secure digital communications. Cryptography has been used for thousands of years. Historical records show that ancient Egyptians used encryption around 4,000 years ago to send secret messages during war. Kings would dispatch encrypted messages to their generals via trusted couriers. A strong cryptographic algorithm is characterized by the complexity of its data processing and its ability to meet the following four essential requirements [11, 12]:

- Confidentiality: Ensures that authorized parties can only access and read the message (plaintext).
- Authentication: Confirms the sender's identity, preventing unauthorized individuals from impersonating others.
- Integrity: Guarantees the message has not been altered or tampered with during transmission.
- Non-Repudiation: Ensures that the sender cannot deny having sent the message. This provides accountability and proof of origin in communication.

Figure 2.1 illustrates the basic process within a cryptographic system. If we represent the message as **M**, the encryption process as **E**, and the key as **K**, then the resulting ciphertext **C** can be expressed as:

$$\mathbf{C} = \mathbf{E}(\mathbf{K}, \mathbf{M}) \tag{2.1}$$

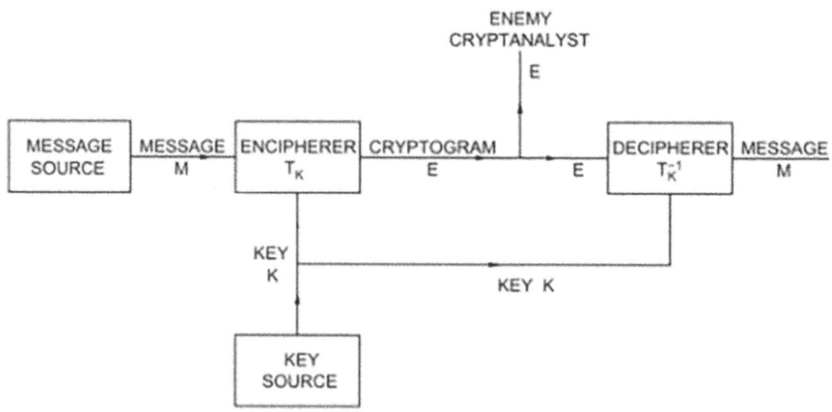

Figure 2.1 Cryptography ecosystem.

Equation 2.1 forms the foundation of all modern symmetric cryptographic algorithms, where the same key is used for both encryption and decryption. A system that follows this structure is commonly referred to as a cryptosystem.

In the early stages of cryptographic development, the security of a method often relied on keeping the algorithm itself secret—a concept known as security through obscurity. However, in 1883, a significant shift occurred when Auguste Kerckhoffs, in a French journal, introduced what is now known as Kerckhoffs's Principle. This principle asserts that the security of a cryptographic system should depend solely on the secrecy of the key, not on the secrecy of the encryption method itself.

Claude Shannon, a pioneer in modern cryptography, emphasized that when designing a cryptosystem, one must assume that the adversary is fully aware of the system's design. This assumption remains a fundamental principle in evaluating the security of cryptographic algorithms today. In the Advanced Encryption Standard (AES) algorithm, both the input (plaintext) and output (ciphertext) are represented as a sequence of 128 bits, grouped into a single unit known as a data block. This block serves as the core unit of encryption. The cipher key used in AES varies depending on the key length—typically 128, 192, or 256 bits. The bits in the data block and key are numbered sequentially from 0 to $n-1$, where n is the total number of bits.

2.2 Literature Review

Technological development plays a crucial role in human life, especially in computer science, which enables the completion of complex tasks quickly and efficiently. This progress, however, is closely linked to the advancement of mathematics, as every technological innovation is underpinned by mathematical calculations and models. Despite its many benefits, technology also brings significant risks. One primary concern is the ease with which confidential data can be accessed or stolen using computers. Modern tools can uncover sensitive information through hacking, data breaches, surveillance, or unauthorized access. Such activities have led to numerous high-profile cases of data theft, including incidents involving LinkedIn, Gmail, and other major platforms [13].

Table 2.1 Comparison of Symmetric Cryptographic Algorithms [15]

CHIPER	KEY MAKE	INFORMATION
Twofish	Bruce schneier	Very strong, widely used
Blowfish	Bruce schneier	Old and slow
Rijndael/AES	Rivest, shamir, and adleman	Best choice
Triple DES	IBM	Second best choice
DES	IBM	Too weak to use now
RC4	Ronald rivest	Caution: some keys are weak
RC5	Ronald rivest	Good but patented
Serpent	Anderson, Biham, Knudsen	Very strong

To address these security challenges, cryptography has emerged as a vital area of computational mathematics focused on protecting information. It ensures data confidentiality, integrity, authenticity, and non-repudiation. The AES is a widely used symmetric encryption algorithm that operates on fixed-size data blocks. It was developed by Vincent Rijmen and Joan Daemen as an improvement over the older Data Encryption Standard (DES), which had become vulnerable—its keys could be cracked in a matter of days using specialized hardware (NIST, 1998) [14].

AES processes 128-bit data blocks and supports key sizes of 128, 192, or 256 bits. Since 2006, AES has been among the most widely adopted symmetric encryption algorithms. Other symmetric algorithms include Blowfish, DES, IDEA, RC4, RC5, Triple DES, Twofish, and Serpent—each with its own strengths and weaknesses, as shown in Table 2.1.

The proposed algorithm uses AES for security purposes. The implementation of this algorithm on digital images has previously been carried out, including the design and implementation of an encryption application. Description of digital photos using the Rijndael Algorithm, which produces encryption and decryption techniques with an accuracy value of 100%, image encryption, and decryption. Using the AES algorithm can encrypt and decrypt an image. An effective AES implementation, which produces the best AES algorithm, is to use a 128-bit key.

2.3 Cryptanalysis

Cryptanalysis (from the Greek kryptós, "hidden", and analýein, let go) is the discipline of reading encrypted messages without knowing any confidential information or keys that should be used to read the message. In everyday language, cryptanalysis is the science of decoding—the disciplines used in cryptography, including mathematics, linguistics, logic, and computer science. Cryptanalysis was first coined by the Arab scientist, the Abbasid caliph al-Kindi. In his book, an inner manuscript, Cracking Cryptographic Messages, he describes in detail the frequency analysis method, which is the basis for cryptanalytic methods. Cryptanalysis continues to develop according to technological developments. One well-known example is the Enigma cryptanalysis machine of World War II [16].

In the mid-1970s, a new group of cryptography emerged called asymmetric cryptography. Basically, all passwords remained vulnerable to cryptanalysis using frequency analysis techniques up to the development of polyalphabetic ciphers, which was described by Leon Battista Alberti around 1467. However, some indications indicate that Al-Kindi had already recognized this. Alberti's discoveries used different ciphers (such as alphabet substitution) for several parts of the message (possibly for each successive text letter until the end). He also discovered what might be a cipher device automatically for the first time; the wheels implemented the execution of his invention. In the polyalphabetic Vigenère cipher, encryption uses a word key, which regulates letter substitution based on which letter of that keyword is used [17].

In the mid-19th century, Charles Babbage pointed out that the Vigenère cipher is particularly vulnerable to Kasiski's examination; however, this was first published about ten years later by Friedrich Kasiski. Although frequency analysis can be very powerful and become a standard technique against many passwords, encryption is still very effective, as much of cryptanalysis is still concerned with its application. Solving messages without using frequency analysis requires password knowledge and maybe the key used, which creates espionage, bribery, theft, etc. This is emphatically admitted; cipher algorithms in the 19th century were very insensitive and did not enforce message security practices; in fact, it is further recognized that each sufficient cryptographic scheme (including passwords) must remain secure, though the enemy was utterly clueless about the cipher algorithm itself [18].

The key holder must be able to guarantee the safety of the key and keep it secret, even when attacked. This fundamental principle was first described in 1883 by Auguste Kerckhoffs and is generally known as the Kerckhoff Principle; alternatively, and bluntly, this point is explained by Claude Shannon, founder of information theory and the fundamentals of cryptography theory, as the Shannon proverb – "the enemy knows the system". Attacks ("cryptanalytic attacks") against cryptography can be grouped in several ways [19, 20, 21, 22]:

- Passive Attack: In this attack, the attacker is not involved in communicating between the sender and receiver, but the attacker intercepts all message exchanges between the two entities. The aim is to obtain as much information as possible for cryptanalysis. Several tapping methods include:
- Wiretapping: Tappers intercept data transmitted on communication cable channels using a hardware connection.
- Electromagnetic Eavesdropping: Eavesdroppers intercept data transmitted over wireless channels, such as radio and microwave. Based on the amount of information known by cryptanalysts, the attacks can be grouped into five types, namely:
- Ciphertext-Only Attack: This is the most common type of attack, but the most difficult, because the information available is only ciphertext. Cryptanalysts have multiple ciphertexts of multiple messages, all encrypted with the same algorithm. For this reason, cryptanalysts use several methods, such as trying all possible keys by exhaustive search and using frequency analysis, making guesses based on known information, and so on.
- Known-Plaintext Attack: This is a type of attack in which the cryptanalyst has a corresponding pair of plaintexts and ciphertext.
- Chosen-Plaintext Attack: This type of attack is more potent than the known-plaintext attack, because cryptanalysts can select the plaintexts they have to encrypt, namely, plaintexts more conducive to key discovery.
- Chosen-Text Attack: This type of attack combines a chosen plaintext attack and a chosen-ciphertext attack. Based on the techniques used in finding the key, the attack can be divided into two, namely:
- Exhaustive Attack or Brute Force Attack: This is an attack to reveal plaintext or keys using all possible keys. It is assumed that the cryptanalyst knows the cryptographic algorithm used

by the message's sender. In addition, cryptanalysts have several ciphertexts and plaintexts that correspond to them.

- Analytical Attack: In this type of attack, the cryptanalyst does not try all possible keys but analyzes the weaknesses of the cryptographic algorithm to reduce the possibility of a missing key. It is assumed that the cryptanalyst knows the cryptographic algorithm used by the message's sender. Analysis can use a mathematical and statistical approach to find the key.
- Related-Key Attack: A Cryptanalyst has a ciphertext encrypted with two different keys. The cryptanalyst does not know the two keys, but he knows the relationship between the two keys, for example, knowing that the two keys are only 1 bit different.
- Rubber-hose Cryptanalysis: This is the most extreme and most effective type of attack. The attacker threatened, sent an illegal letter, or tortured him until the person holding the key gave him the key to decrypt the message. For cryptanalysis of the Vigenere cipher itself, the first step to solving the ciphertext key is to determine its length. Several methods are used to solve the key length, including the frequency and the case test. Cryptanalysis can be done in a variety of languages around the world, but only a few have been solved and analyzed. In addition, cryptanalysis is not perfect in solving a ciphertext; therefore, a probability value is taken, often called the coincidence index. Coincidence index is a relationship between one letter and another letter that can produce the possibility of a key. The formula in Equation 2.2 is used for finding the coincidence index as follows:

$$I_c(x) = \frac{\sum_{i=0}^{25} f_i (f_i - 1)}{n(n-1)} \tag{2.2}$$

$\boldsymbol{I_c}$ = Coincidence Index
$\boldsymbol{f_i}$ = Frequencies of A, B, C..., Z
$\boldsymbol{n}$ = The number of characters of the entire ciphertext text

2.4 Problem Formulation

Based on the background of the problem and the focus of the research, it is necessary to formulate the problem briefly as follows:

- How is the electronic transaction mechanism (e-commerce) through the internet payment system done?
- How about electronic transactions (e-commerce) through an internet payment system, according to the IT Act of 2000 on consumer information protection?
- What is the test result of the encrypted and decrypted data against the attack?

2.4.1 *Proposed Work and Algorithm*

The workflow model in Figure 2.2 depicts the functional scenario of the proposed scheme. While communicating with the server resource over the network, the e-commerce-based mobile application will encrypt the credentials or any transaction on the client resource. Thereafter, the encrypted value will be sent over the network. Subsequently, the same will be read on the server or application-server resource using a port and decrypted to its original value or plaintext for further processing and computing.

2.4.2 *Proposed Algorithm*

The proposed algorithm process starts with encryption. Authors have to select or attain the value to encrypt; for example, we can opt for any value, let's say COLOUR to encrypt. The following steps elaborate on the encryption process-

1. Every value or character has a decimal number; therefore, under the proposed scheme, each character value will be converted to an American Standard Code for Information Interchange (ASCII) decimal value.

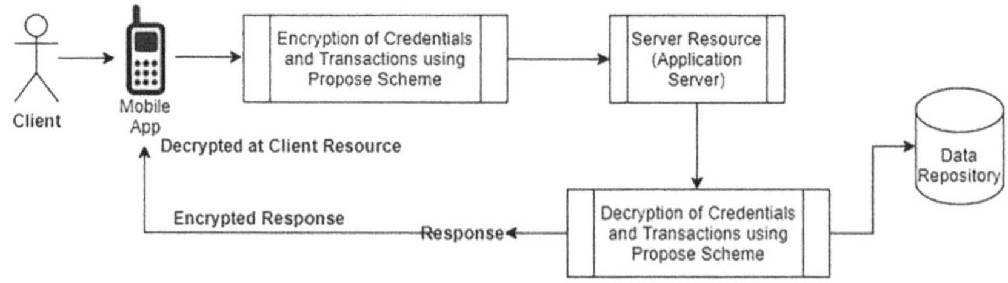

Figure 2.2 Workflow model of proposed scheme.

2. Adding a random (15) value to each ASCII value achieved in Step 1.
3. Prefixing zeros based on certain conditions.
   a. If the value is less than 10, the same will be prefixed with 00. For example, if the value is 5, the same should be converted to 005.
   b. If the value is less than 100, the same will be prefixed with 0, for example, if the value is 50, the same should be converted to 050.
   c. If the value is greater than 100, the value will remain the same; for example, if the value is 105, the value will remain as 105.
   d. After prefixing the zeros, reverse the last output values.
4. In this step, we will attain a symmetric key, an arbitrary number of non-redundant 10-digit numbers ranging from 0 to 9.
5. Now, under step 4, again, we will reverse the value.
6. Inculcating XOR substitution with another key enhances security, assuming that another arbitrary key is formed.
7. Thereafter, an exponential form will be created with respect to every reversed value, and the value is reversed to form a more complicated structure.

The reverse of the encryption function is used to decrypt the substitution cipher. The decryption of the substitution cipher only changes the inverse from the inverse process of the encryption process, so that the key used is symmetrical or the same as the encryption process.

2.4.3 Testing Environment

The proposed algorithm is evaluated based on the time taken, as shown in Table 2.2 and Figure 2.3.

Table 2.2 represents the time Central Processing Unit (CPU) consumed in seconds/milliseconds in the proposed scheme. The time is

Table 2.2 Time (CPU) in Seconds/Milliseconds

MACHINE	CPU TIME IN SECONDS
1	1.21
2	0.923

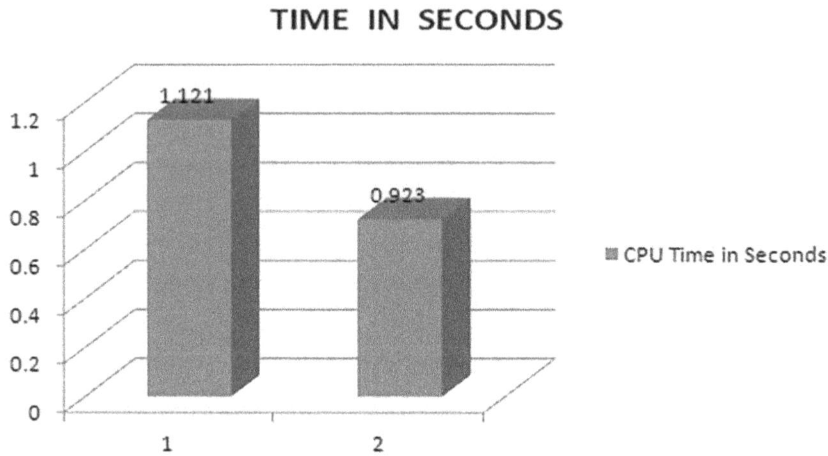

Figure 2.3 Time taken by the proposed algorithm.

satisfactory for the proposed work. It takes almost 1 second to encrypt and decrypt the secret data.

Figure 2.3 plot using a bar depicting the efficiency and time used to encrypt and decrypt the proposed scheme. The results demonstrate that the proposed algorithm is computationally efficient, requiring minimal resources for execution. Therefore, the algorithm performs well within a reasonable time and is computationally robust.

2.5 Conclusion

The proposed substitution cipher algorithm has encryption characters that are relatively simple and easy because they are based on existing tables that are safe enough to guarantee confidentiality. After all, the characters of the encrypted plaintext letters are not the same as the resulting ciphertext. This is one of the advantages of the substitution algorithm. The algorithm's ciphertext is not the same as its plaintext and its solution because it is considered difficult for laymen if the character of this algorithm is long.

The proposed substitution cipher algorithm depends on selecting the keys used in the encryption process. If the key is long, then the required process will be longer to crack a ciphertext, which may require good computational power and time. The deep cryptanalysis of this proposed cipher algorithm combines two keys (Symmetric and

XOR). So, finding the key's length gets a very low probability and high confidentiality.

References

[1] Song, Y., Wu, Q., Wang, X., Wang, C., & Miao, X. (2021). Two memristor-based XOR logic demonstrated with encryption/decryption. *IEEE Electron Device Letters*, *42*(9), 1398–1401.

[2] Protic, D., & Stankovic, M. (2023). XOR-based detector of different decisions on anomalies in the computer network traffic. *Science and Technology*, *26*(3–4), 323–338.

[3] Fard, S. S., Kaveh, M., Mosavi, M. R., & Ko, S. B. (2022). An efficient modeling attack for breaking the security of XOR-Arbiter PUFs by using the fully connected and long-short term memory. *Microprocessors and Microsystems*, *94*, 104667.

[4] Bernasconi, A., Cimato, S., Ciriani, V., & Molteni, M. C. (2022). Multiplicative complexity of XOR-based regular functions. *IEEE Transactions on Computers*, *71*(11), 2927–2939.

[5] Tan, J., Wu, Z., & Chen, L. (2025). New Bayesian estimation method based on symmetric projection space and particle flow velocity. *Symmetry*, *17*(6), 899.

[6] Shi, X., Sun, J., Xiao, X., Zhang, Y., Lei, Y., Yang, H., & Li, Z. (2025). A load restoration approach based on symmetrical demand response incentive mechanism. *Energies*, *18*(11), 2677.

[7] Al-Zubaidie, M., & Shyaa, G. S. (2023). Applying detection leakage on hybrid cryptography to secure transaction information in e-commerce apps. *Future Internet*, *15*(8), 262.

[8] Bhatia, N. L., Shukla, V. K., Punhani, R., & Dubey, S. K. (2021, June). Growing aspects of cybersecurity in e-commerce. In *2021 International Conference on Communication information and Computing Technology* (pp. 1–6). IEEE.

[9] Cebeci, S. E., Nari, K., & Ozdemir, E. (2022). Secure e-commerce scheme. *IEEE Access*, *10*, 10359–10370.

[10] Kim, S. I., & Kim, S. H. (2022). E-commerce payment model using blockchain. *Journal of Ambient Intelligence and Humanized Computing*, *13*(3), 1673–1685.

[11] Markavathi, J. N. P., Pandiarajan, R., & Jaya Priyangaa, R.M. (2025, April). End-to-end secure cryptographic system. In *2024 International Conference on IT Innovation and Knowledge Discovery* (pp. 1–7). IEEE.

[12] Süzen, A. A., & Duman, B. (2021). Blockchain-based secure credit card storage system for e-commerce. *Sakarya University Journal of Computer and Information Sciences*, *4*(2), 204–215.

[13] Khurana, R. (2022). Applications of quantum computing in telecom e-commerce: Analysis of qkd, qaoa, and qml for data encryption, speed optimization, and ai-driven customer experience. *Quarterly Journal of Emerging Technologies and Innovations*, *7*(9), 1–15.

[14] Kovalchuk, O., Shevchuk, R., & Banakh, S. (2024). *Cryptocurrency crime risks modeling: Environment, e-commerce, and cybersecurity issue. IEEE Access.*

[15] Jiang, T., Yuan, X., Cheng, Q., Shen, Y., Wang, L., & Ma, J. (2023). FairECom: Towards proof of e-commerce fairness against price discrimination. *IEEE Transactions on Dependable and Secure Computing, 21*(4), 3528–3544.

[16] Wang, Z. (2025). Cryptanalysis in e-commerce: A novel arrangement procedure using DHEC-SAT upon elliptic curve cryptography. *Multimedia Tools & Applications, 84*(8), 5377–5395.

[17] Das, M., & Chakraborty, R. (2022, September). Statistical cryptanalysis of ElGamal cryptosystem for measuring security in disruptive technology. In *2022 Second International Conference on Computer Science, Engineering and Applications* (pp. 1–5). IEEE.

[18] Oliveira, S., Leal, A. B., Teixeira, M., & Lopes, Y. K. (2023, August). Security of cyber-physical systems against actuator attacks through cryptography. In *2023 International Conference on Information Technology* (pp. 758–764). IEEE.

[19] Thabit, F., Can, O., Aljahdali, A. O., Al-Gaphari, G. H., & Alkhzaimi, H. A. (2023). Cryptography algorithms for enhancing IoT security. *Internet of Things, 22*, 100759.

[20] Khalid, Z. M., & Askar, S. (2021). Resistant blockchain cryptography to quantum computing attacks. *International Journal of Science and Business, 5*(3), 116–125.

[21] Shaller, A., Zamir, L., & Nojoumian, M. (2023). Roadmap of post-quantum cryptography standardization: Side-channel attacks and countermeasures. *Information and Computation, 295*, 105112.

[22] Pilania, U., Kumar, M., Singh, S., Futela, S., & Jha, N. (2023, December). A text encryption approach for IoT devices to prioritize security and efficiency. In *International Conference on Advancements in Smart Computing and Information Security* (pp. 62–70). Springer Nature Switzerland.

3

Image Steganography

Techniques, Applications, and Future Directions

3.1 Introduction

Within the realm of image files, image steganography is defined as the method used to store information so that concealing the fact that data is stored in the image becomes impossible. It differs from cryptography, which disorganizes the message to protect it from unwanted devices. Unlike cryptography, steganography attempts to obscure the message by embedding the clues within some cover medium, often a picture. This method takes advantage of the ever-increasing amount of redundant data in images, especially high-resolution ones.

Furthermore, with the increase in digital information and its fast-paced circulation, steganography serves many purposes, including secure communication, information verification, watermarking, and storage of sensitive information. Various techniques have been developed for embedding data, extending from simple spatial domain methods such as Least Significant Bit (LSB) substitution to sophisticated ones like Discrete Cosine Transform (DCT) and Discrete Wavelet Transform (DWT) for transform domain methods. As new digital threats arise, the need for image steganography as a source of information protection from interception, alteration, and exposure without permission becomes more essential.

Figure 3.1 illustrates the types of steganography based on the Domain and the key evaluation parameters. Payload refers to the volume of information that can be hidden without noticeably affecting the quality of the stego file. Imperceptibility indicates how visually similar the stego file is to the original; the higher the imperceptibility, the

DOI: 10.1201/9781003504139-3

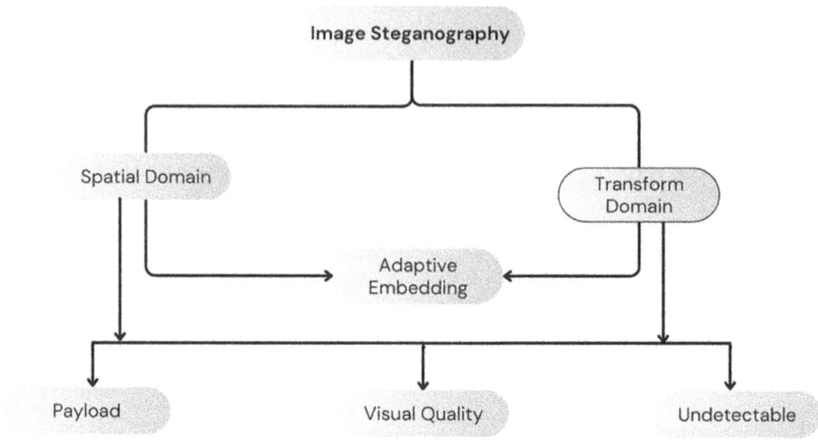

Figure 3.1 Evaluation parameters.

lower the likelihood of detecting the concealed message. If the hidden information remains undetectable, it suggests that the proposed technique is robust enough to withstand several image-processing attacks.

Image steganography finds applications across various domains, including secure information exchange in military operations, digital rights management, protection of medical records, and covert communication. While several steganalysis techniques have been developed to detect hidden data, the increasing complexity of image data poses significant challenges to detection. These complex patterns enable high data-hiding capacity, resilience against image-processing attacks, and compatibility with emerging data formats. This review chapter provides an in-depth overview of existing image-steganography techniques, their effectiveness, prevailing trends, and ongoing challenges. It also explores future directions involving artificial intelligence (AI), quantum computing, and blockchain technologies. The primary objective of the chapter is to identify research gaps and support future innovations in information security.

3.2 Literature Review

Steganography is one of the techniques for data concealing, in which invisible communication is usually concerned with the way in which the existence of the communicated message may be hidden. In the case of steganography, information can be concealed in various embedding media, referred to as carriers. These carriers can include image, audio, video, and text data. This chapter examines the consideration of an image file as a carrier, and thus, the classification schemes of current steganography methods for image files have been outlined. These methods are discussed not only for the capability of concealing information in image files but also for the volume of information concealment possible and the strength against various image-processing pseudorandom attacks [1].

As multiple public channels disseminate information, transmission over them becomes highly interesting because of their potential value. Data security is one of the primary concerns in today's digital world, and there are different ways of achieving security. Multimedia data, such as images, requires encryption methods more than anything else. A significant problem of image encryption is that, although the encrypted images are useless for several applications, an adversary can easily tell that an image contains encrypted data. To address this issue, techniques such as steganography and watermarking have been developed. With steganography, secret information is concealed beneath the surface of an ordinary image in such a way that it cannot be noticed. A significant aspect of image steganography is its statistical model, since it allows for the estimation of the location of the least significant bits that could be modified without changing the image to attain better protection. This chapter seeks to offer dedicated approaches to image steganography, which has market relevance [2].

Many techniques exist to conceal a particular piece of information within images. The central issue is to enhance the concealing capacity so that no one is aware of the existence of secret data. In the proposed work [3], Invertible Steganography Network (ISN) has been used for concealing secret data into images. The goal of image steganography is to embed one or more images within a host image so that concealment is achieved and restoration is possible at any point in time. Prior image-steganography techniques are limited in the amount of information they can embed and their robustness, and they are often exposed to attacks on cover images. In the proposed work, invertible image steganography based on RIIS has been utilized [4]. Conditional normalizing flow has been applied to the high-frequency component of the cover image. Work was evaluated based on various performance parameters such as concealing capacity, imperceptibility, and robustness against attacks.

The existing image steganography methods focus on cover-based techniques, which tend to have the problem of secret image disclosure and weak robustness toward lossy degradation of the container images. Recent advancements in the diffusion models gave us the idea that some properties of diffusion models, such as unconditioned image-to-image adaptations and robustness to noisy images, could enhance security and natural robustness for image steganography. For the diffusion model, the author took the conditional diffusion model, Stable Diffusion, and took advantage of LoRAs and ControlNets from open-source communities to increase the manageability and variety of the images used as cover images. Therefore, the authors presented a novel image steganography framework, Controllable, Robust and Secure Image Steganography (CRoSS), which outperforms cover-based image steganography in controllability, robustness, and security, and these features are attained without further training. This is the initial study that leverages diffusion models for image steganography. In the experimental part, the author provided a set of experiments designed specifically to validate the CRoSS framework regarding controllability, robustness, and security [5].

The Deep Learning (DL) techniques for image steganography are emerging these days, but have shown great promise recently. Yet, there are gaps in the research about DL-based steganography. In the work, authors presented a novel end-to-end generative adversarial framework for image steganography with channel attention mechanisms that can produce indistinguishable stego images of different capacities. The proposed model comprises three subnetworks: a cover image generator, a device that extracts information from stego images , and a steganography security enhancer that functions as a discriminator. The authors proposed a special channel attention module designed to exploit interdependencies of channels to tune channel-wise features in images' deep representations. The simulation of the proposed work validates that the channel attention strategy is favorable to the quality of generated stego images and retrieved stego image quality. To handle these issues, authors incorporate extractable error-correction codes, enabling our model to achieve maximum effective embedding rates over 4 bits per pixel [6].

Images have always been an ideal medium for concealing information using steganography techniques. Any data, whether it a message, a document, or another image, can easily be hidden within the bitmap of a digital picture with no human detection. Until now, there has been a vast amount of literature combining many methods providing various steganography techniques and steganalysis methods, which are used to find hidden information in data files. Modern steganography methods usually use Convolutional Neural Networks (CNNs) that try to embed vast amounts of information into images with as little visible change as possible. This article intends to illustrate that a Generative Adversarial Network (GAN) could enhance the concealment effectiveness of a spatial-domain steganography technique while minimizing the changes made to the picture. During the training phase, the GAN is taught how to modify an image in a way that makes it possible to embed a message later through the LSB steganography algorithm. Results show that the method successfully avoids detection by an advanced DL-based steganalysis system [7].

3.3 Classification of Image Steganography

Spatial-domain techniques modify the pixel values of an image directly to hide information within the cover image. Their simplicity, efficiency, and high payload capacity make these methods popular. One of the most widely known methods is the LSB substitution, where the least significant bits of the pixel values are substituted by bits from the secret data. Because of the changes made to the least significant bits, this method ensures LSB-based imperceptibility benefits. Another well-known technique is Pixel Value Differencing (PVD), where data is embedded based on the difference between the values of two adjacent pixels.

On the other hand, edge-based embedding methods embed the information on the edges detected by edge detection algorithms in high-frequency areas of the image, where the changes are less visible to the naked eye. Although easy to implement, such spatial-domain methods are more vulnerable to image-processing actions such as compression, filtering, or resizing. In short, speed and capacity advantages make spatial-domain techniques appealing, but they require resilience mechanisms. Figure 3.2 represents a type of steganography based on the spatial and transform domains. Which are further divided into subparts.

In the graphical aspect of image steganography, particularly in the spatial Domain, the LSB technique is arguably the simplest and most famous method. It conceals secret data in images by substituting the least significant bits of a pixel with the message to be hidden. Due to its insignificant nature, modifying the LSB of a pixel will not change the image in any meaningful way. The LSB of the pixel's intensity can be altered without a noticeable difference in the resultant image. A good example is an 8-bit grayscale image, changing the LSBs modifies the intensity by one.

The sufficient bandwidth of color images means information can be concealed within the LSBs of the red, green, and blue channels. Even with these advantages, the simplicity and high capacity of LSB method is offset by crippling weaknesses. The ability to hide data without detection is negated by the ease with which hidden data can be destroyed by compression, cropping, and adding noise. Furthermore, LSB embedding is exposed to steganalysis mechanisms that predictably use statistical methods to uncover hidden data. To increase robustness and security, techniques such as random pixel selection, multi-bit LSB, and encryption of hidden data can be added.

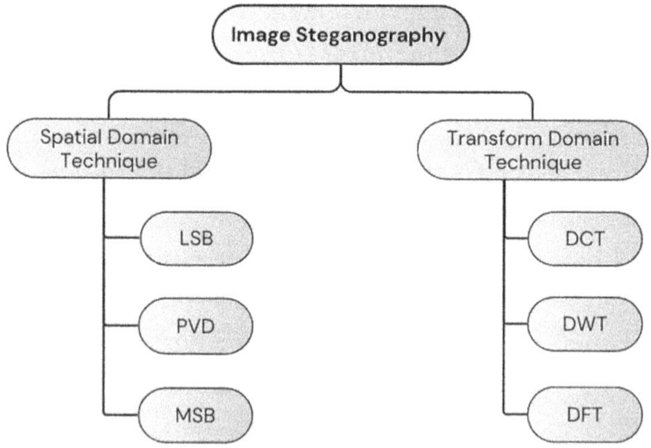

Figure 3.2 Steganography based on domain.

Despite that, LSB is still a basic technique used in steganography owing to its simplicity in implementation. Figure 3.3 illustrates how LSB steganography works. A secret message, "DOG," is hidden within the cover image, resulting in the creation of a stego image. The LSBs of the cover image are replaced by the bits of the secret message, with the modified bits highlighted in red. At the receiver's end, the process is reversed to extract the hidden message from the stego image. Although LSB steganography is straightforward and fast, its simplicity makes it relatively easy to detect the concealed message within the stego file. It is not robust against image-processing attacks and can be detected during the compression of the stego file.

PVD is an advanced form of steganography, and spatial-domain image techniques have been developed to improve some drawbacks

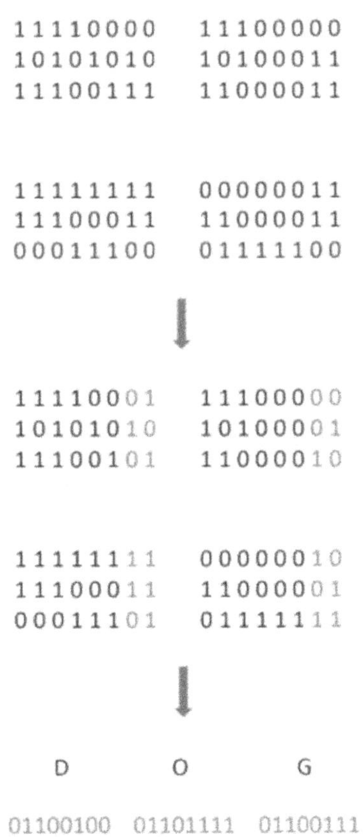

Figure 3.3 LSB steganography process.

posed by methods like LSB substitution. PVD processes the image into non-overlapping pairs of adjacent pixels, calculating the difference between the intensity values. This difference will dictate how many bits can be hidden in that pixel pair. In high-contrast regions or areas where there are edges and the pixel differences are large, more information can be concealed because such changes will hardly be detected by the human eye viewing the image. Smooth areas with low pixel differences give smaller bits to hide information without being detected. It is this adaptability that makes PVD have a better balance of payload capacity and visual render beneath the surface.

PVD also has better protection against visual and statistical attacks when compared to simple LSB methods. Unfortunately, image-processing operations such as compression or filtering may create vulnerabilities within PVD, and care must be taken to protect the embedding process by maintaining proper bounds within the pixel value ranges post-embedding. Regardless, PVD is widely recognized as a robust and efficient image data hiding technique, especially when enhanced with other methods to strengthen security and resilience.

Most Significant Bit (MSB) steganography is a more detectable and primitive way of concealing information within images by changing the most significant bits of pixel values, as shown in Figure 3.4. Unlike the LSB method, which steganographically modifies the less critical bits, MSB steganography overwrites the bits with a significant influence on the pixel with an intensity value, rendering them visually detectable. For example, in an 8-bit grayscale image, overwriting the MSB results in high pixel values, which generate a considerable change in brightness and introduce artifacts in the picture. Any such images created in watermarking can have their image attributes changed without consequence. Table 3.1 represents the difference between spatial-domain steganography techniques.

In MSB steganography, the secret message is embedded in the most significant bits of the cover image. As shown in the figure, the MSB bits are replaced with the bits of the secret message, highlighted in red. At the receiver's end, the hidden message is extracted from the stego file. Unlike LSB steganography, changes to the cover image can be more noticeable due to the alteration of the most significant bits. However, this method remains simple and faster compared to techniques like PVD and other similar approaches.

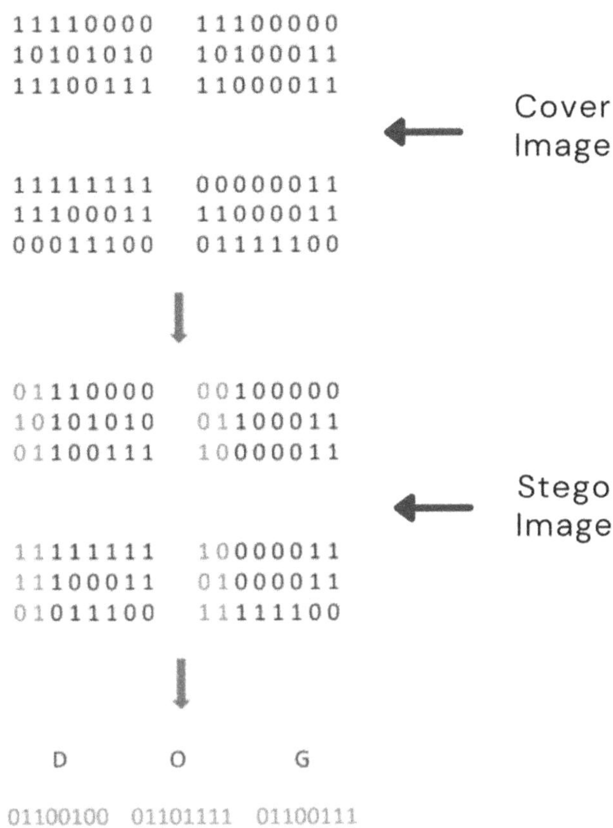

Figure 3.4 MSB steganography process.

Transform-domain techniques in image steganography are about hiding secret data in the frequency components of an image rather than the visual pixel values. With these methods, the mathematical transformation of an image to the spatial domain and later from the spatial domain to the frequency domain is done so that some portions of the image, less sensitive to compression, noise, or distortion, can be used to hide data in steganography. One of the most popular techniques is called DCT. The DCT is used in Joint Photographic Experts Group (JPEG) compression and in DCT-based steganography; the secret data is hidden in the middle-frequency coefficients of image blocks. This is a tradeoff between imperceptibility and robustness. Another strong method is the DWT, which decomposes the image into several sub-bands at various levels. DWT also helps conceal other information by embedding hidden

Table 3.1 Difference between Spatial-Domain Steganography

PARAMETER	LSB	MSB	PVD
Bit Positioning	Data is concealed in the least significant bits of the cover file	Data is hidden in the most significant bits of the cover file	Data is concealed based on the difference in neighboring pixel values
Visual Quality	On concealing extensive amounts of data, the visual quality degrades	Low visual quality as data is hidden in the most significant bits, which affects most.	Visual quality is high as the region is selected based on a significant pixel difference.
Concealing Amount	Good, but it may result in degradation of the stego file when more data is hidden.	Low compared to the LSB	Concealing capacity depends on local variations in pixel values
Robustness against Attacks	It is not robust against a compression attack	Less robust when more data is hidden	It is robust against basic attacks.
Security of Secret Data	It is simple to implement, and it is easy to detect hidden secret data	Less secure compared to LSB	It is not predictable, so it is more secure
Quality of Cover	Good	Poor	Good
Complexity	It is a simple technique to implement	It is the simplest, but not so practical	It requires analysis of neighboring pixel pairs
Data Concealing Approach	Substitutes LSBs with secret data bits	Substitutes MSB bits with secret data bits	It conceals bits by calculating the pixel intensity difference in neighboring pixels.
Applications	It works well with the image cover file	It is most suitable for visible watermarking	It hides data based on the textures or edges of the cover image

data in high-frequency sub-bands, which are difficult to detect but maintain image quality easily. The less common Fourier transform is used for embedding data into repeating designed spaces within an image. This approach is not as popular because it is more complicated. Transform domain techniques are more robust than spatial methods for widespread attacks like compression, filtering, and geometric distortions [8].

Nevertheless, their computational expense is exceptionally high, and they typically have a smaller payload capacity. Recently, hybrid approaches that blend different transform techniques, such as DWT–DCT, have emerged to use the strengths from multiple domains better and achieve a more optimal balance between imperceptibility, robustness, and capacity. With these developments, transform-domain steganography is the most effective for highly secured and resilient applications [9].

The DCT is one of the conventional transform-domain processes in image steganography; it works well on JPEG images. DCT converts an image from the spatial domain into the frequency domain by decomposing it into blocks and transforming each block into multiple frequency coefficients. Different frequencies interpret various aspects of the image; low frequencies contain a general overview of the image, while high frequencies contain finer details. In DCT-based steganography, secret information is usually inserted into the middle-frequency coefficients of the modified images. This method leaves the low- and high- frequency components, which are crucial for compression visual perception, largely unaltered.

Moderate middle-frequency coefficient alterations provide a good balance between imperceptibility and robustness in DCT steganography. After embedding, an image is inverse transformed after applying DCT to reconstruct the image. One main disadvantage concerning the DCT method is its increased sensitivity to lossy compression, like JPEG, rendering it unfit for industrial concerns where image quality and integrity are of prime consideration. In any case, the technique is more demanding of processing resources than spatial-domain techniques and tends to offer lower payload capacity. DCT remains a primary pillar of watermarked image steganography, constantly refined through hybrid methods and adaptive algorithms [10].

Widely used as part of a transform-domain technique in image steganography, DWT is one of the most effective due to its capability of representing both spatial and frequency domains at once. Steganography image files can be broken down using DWT into several sub-bands, which are usually named LL (low–low), LH (low–high), HL (high–low), and HH (high–high). These sub-bands in turn contain different ranges of frequencies and orientation. The LL sub-band holds both the image approximation and most of the energy. The other sub-bands hold essential details such as edge and texture. In most steganography models, secret data are hidden in LH, HL, or HH sub-bands because they lower the perceptual power distortion [11]. DWT has benefits such as being more robust against compression and image processing attacks, being more imperceptible, and allowing for multi-resolution analysis, making it suitable for adaptive and scalable data hiding. Also, it is common for DWT to be combined with other transforms like the DCT or Singular Value Decomposition (SVD) in hybrid methods to boost performance. DWT techniques, however, are more complex computationally and may have less data embedding capacity than the spatial-domain methods [12].

In Discrete Fourier Transformation (DFT)-based steganography, images are first decomposed into blocks, which are then transformed into the frequency domain. After which, secret information is concealed in the image by altering the magnitude of specific frequency components, typically low regions of the image, enabling better quality image preservation [13]. Steganography hides messages inside images; the message is embedded into bitrate chunks by manipulating it with a mathematical process, transforming it from spatial data into sinusoidal frequency representations. Instead of relying solely on cosines like DCT does, DFT utilizes both sine and cosine, yielding complex numbers that encompass magnitude and phase image frequencies. The advantages by using DFT are that it is robust with geometric distortions (rotation, scale, and translation) as the phase is less sensitive to rotation, scale and translation. These properties make DFT suitable for watermarking and applications in which resistance to manipulation is essential. However, DFT is more complex by using complex numbers and is less used for high-capacity data hiding because of its payload capacity limitation [14]. The difference between transform-domain steganography is shown in Table 3.2.

3.4 Applications of Image Steganography

Steganography has its application in various fields. Some of its applications are given as follows in Figure 3.5 [15, 16, 17].

- It is most commonly used for transforming sensitive data so that no one knows its existence.
- It protects copyright or ownership data by concealing it in digital multimedia.
- It ensures the safety and integrity of medical data by concealing patients' sensitive data.
- It provides authentication and integrity to secret data by concealing sensitive data in digital content.
- It is most commonly used in banking applications to add security.

Table 3.2 Differences between Transform-Domain Steganography

PARAMETER	DCT	DFT	DWT
Domain	It hides data in the frequency domain using the cosine function	It hides data in the frequency domain using sine and cosine functions	It hides data in the time-frequency domain using multi-resolution
Basis Functions for Data Hiding	Cosine	Sine and cosine	Wavelets like Haar and Daubechies
Sensitivity	It is comfortable to work with JPEG compressed images	It is sensitive to noise and image modification	It is more robust to noise and compression
Position for Data Hiding	Middle-frequency coefficients are used to conceal secret data	The magnitude or phase of frequency components is selected to conceal secret data	High-frequency sub-bands are chosen to conceal secret data
Robustness	It is the most straightforward technique among the mentioned techniques, so hidden information is easy to detect	In it, concealed data is not easily detectable. So it is robust against some attacks.	It is more robust against attacks.
Compression Ability	JPEG compression uses DCT, so that after data hiding, the size of the cover file does not change	DFT supports compression, but only to a minimal extent; otherwise, the secret message may be detected	It has high compression capacity, and JPEG2000 uses DWT for compression
Computational Efficiency	It requires more computational time and resources	It does not require high computational power	It requires more computational time and resources
Visual Quality	High (when embedding in middle frequencies)	Moderate	High (due to spatial-frequency localization)
Applications	Watermarking, JPEG image steganography	Signal processing, audio/image watermarking	High-performance steganography, medical imaging, JPEG2000

- It is also used in gaming and multimedia for hiding information like cheat codes, developer messages, and watermarking within game assets.
- It is also used in corporate confidential information transmissions.

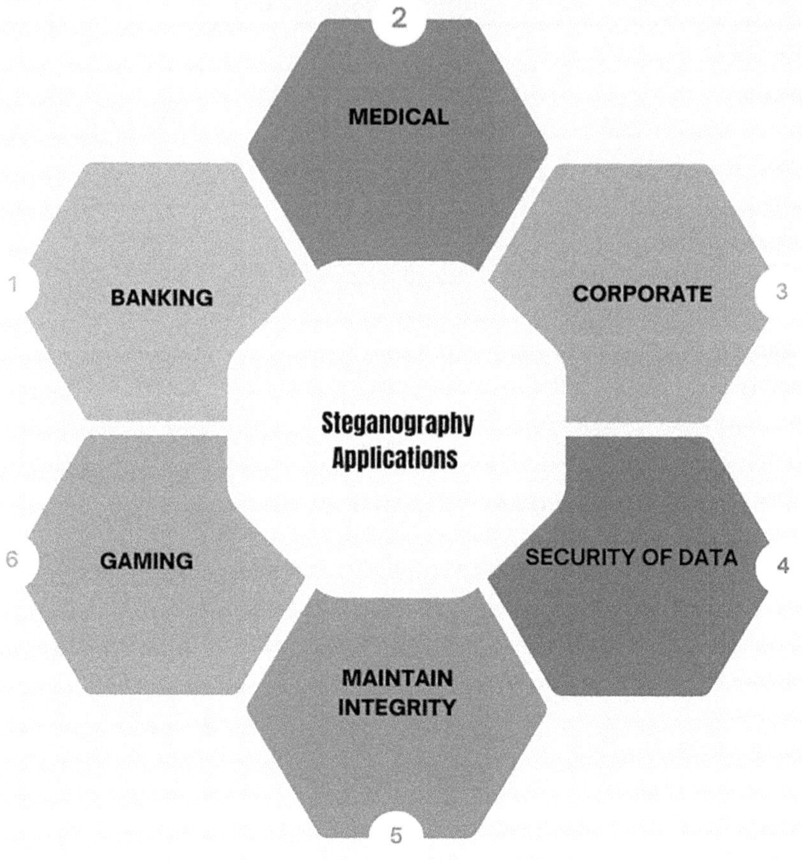

Figure 3.5 Applications of steganography.

3.5 Conclusion

It has been concluded from the literature review that image steganography is a powerful technique for protecting data by embedding hidden information within digital images, which enables covert communication and protects the information from hackers' eyes. Numerous methods, from the basic LSB spatial-domain technique to more advanced DCT and DWT transform domain techniques, provide varying degrees of imperceptibility, strength, and capacity, which makes each of them advantageous. Spatial-domain techniques, while fast and simple, are susceptible to image processing attacks like noise, rotation, transformation, reflection, and compression. The DCT,

DWT, and DFT transform-domain techniques, on the other hand, are incredibly resistant to attack and severe compression, although they result in higher cost and slower computation speed.

References

[1] Hamid, N., Yahya, A., Ahmad, R. B., & Al-Qershi, O. M. (2012). Image steganography techniques: An overview. *International Journal of Computer Science and Security*, *6*(3), 168–187.

[2] Kaur, S., Singh, S., Kaur, M., & Lee, H. N. (2022). A systematic review of computational image steganography approaches. *Archives of Computational Methods in Engineering*, *29*(7), 4775–4797.

[3] Lu, S. P., Wang, R., Zhong, T., & Rosin, P. L. (2021). Large-capacity image steganography based on invertible neural networks. In *Proceedings of the IEEE/CVF Conference onCcomputer Vision and Pattern Recognition* (pp. 10816–10825).

[4] Xu, Y., Mou, C., Hu, Y., Xie, J., & Zhang, J. (2022). Robust invertible image steganography. In *Proceedings of the IEEE/CVF Conference on Computer Vision and Pattern Recognition* (pp. 7875–7884).

[5] Yu, J., Zhang, X., Xu, Y., & Zhang, J. (2023). Cross: The diffusion model makes controllable, robust, and secure image steganography. *Advances in Neural Information Processing Systems*, *36*, 80730–80743.

[6] Tan, J., Liao, X., Liu, J., Cao, Y., & Jiang, H. (2021). Channel attention image steganography with generative adversarial networks. *IEEE Transactions on Network Science and Engineering*, *9*(2), 888–903.

[7] Martín, A., Hernández, A., Alazab, M., Jung, J., & Camacho, D. (2023). Evolving generative adversarial networks to improve image steganography. *Expert Systems with Applications*, *222*, 119841.

[8] Kumar, A., Rani, R., & Singh, S. (2023). A survey of recent advances in image steganography. *Security and Privacy*, *6*(3), e281.

[9] Yao, Y., Wang, J., Chang, Q., Ren, Y., & Meng, W. (2024). High invisibility image steganography with wavelet transform and generative adversarial network—*Expert. Systems with Applications*, *249*, 123540.

[10] Garg, M., Ubhi, J. S., & Aggarwal, A. K. (2023). Neural style transfer for image steganography and destylization with supervised image-to-image translation. *Multimedia Tools andApplications*, *82*(4), 6271–6288.

[11] Yang, H., Xu, Y., Liu, X., & Ma, X. (2024). PRIS: Practical robust invertible network for image steganography. *Engineering Applications of Artificial Intelligence*, *133*, 108419.

[12] Wang, T., Cheng, H., Liu, X., Xu, Y., Chen, F., Wang, M., & Chen, J. (2024). Lossless image steganography: Regard steganography as super-resolution. *Information Processing & Management*, *61*(4), 103719.

[13] Abdulla, A. A. (2024). Digital image steganography: challenges, investigation, and recommendations for the future direction. *Soft Computing*, *28*(15), 8963–8976.

[14] Kumar, V., Sharma, S., Kumar, C., & Sahu, A. K. (2023). Latest trends in deep learning techniques for image steganography. *International Journal of Digital Crime and Forensics*, *15*(1), 1–14.

[15] Pilania, U., & Gupta, P. (2020). Analysis and implementation of the IWT-SVD scheme for video steganography. In *Micro-Electronics and Telecommunication Engineering: Proceedings of 3rd ICMETE 2019* (pp. 153–162). Springer Singapore.

[16] Pilania, U., Tanwar, R., & Gupta, P. (2021). Stable high-capacity video steganography in the wavelet domain. *Turkish Journal of Computer and Mathematics Education*, *12*(7), 2142–2158.

[17] Pilania, U., Kumar, M., Rohit, T., & Nandal, N. (2023). A walk-through towards network steganography techniques. *Informatics and Automation*, *22*(5), 1103–1151.

4

Digital Watermarking Techniques for Multimedia Security

Challenges, Emerging Trends, and Future Directions

4.1 Introduction

The rapid growth of digital media and its widespread use on the internet has revolutionized the way of making, sharing, and consuming information. While this change has brought many benefits, it has also brought important challenges related to unauthorized use, copying, and manipulation of digital materials. Since digital multimedia content, such as images, audio and video files, and documents, can be easily copied and modified without noticeable loss of quality. It requires a pressure of technologies to protect intellectual property and ensure the authenticity of materials [1].

Digital watermarking technology emerged as a solution to problems arising from safety and copyright violations. Creating a watermark involves embedding certain digital signs in a file that ensures the claim, authenticity, tracking, and tampering evaluation. Contrary to encryption, which restricts, watermarking materials allows continuous protection even after being decrypted or distributed. Depending on the objectives, various techniques have been developed in recent decades. There is a general classification of watermarking techniques, which separates them according to the domain in which the watermark is embedded: spatial domains or transform domains. It has intended

DOI: 10.1201/9781003504139-4

objectives, such as copyright security, content authentication, or broadcasting monitoring [2, 3].

Figure 4.1 illustrates the watermarking process, which consists of five stages. In Stage 1, the original image is used as the cover file. In Stage 2, a watermark and an appropriate watermarking algorithm are selected. If the generated watermark is of low quality, it becomes more vulnerable to attacks. At the receiver's end, a watermark detection algorithm is applied to extract the secret message. The basic ideas, varieties, benefits, and boundaries of digital watermarking techniques have been exposed in the review of this chapter. It also discusses the current problems and possibilities of the field for the future and provides a comparative analysis of key approaches. This review helps professionals and researchers identify areas that are ready for multimedia safety progress and select appropriate techniques by compiling existing research.

4.2 Watermark Types

Depending on their purpose, visibility, and ability to change, the watermark can be classified into a variety of types. This is the main difference between visible and invisible watermarks. To establish ownership and prevent illegal use, visible watermarks – which appear to the naked eye – are usually displayed as texts or logos on digital materials

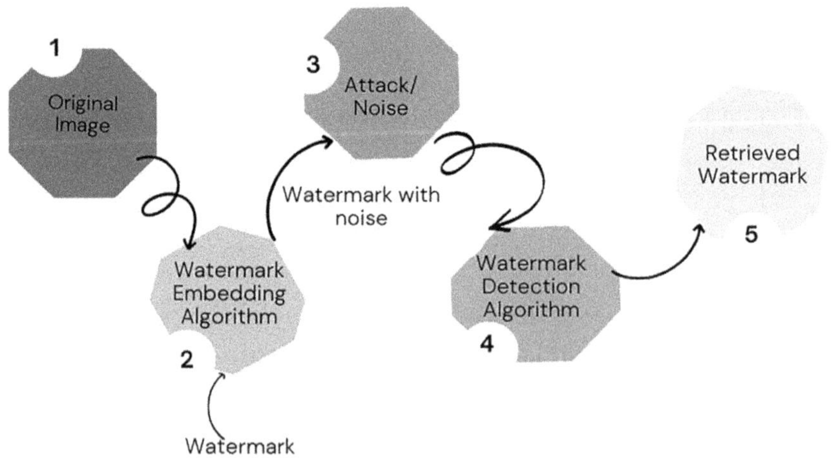

Figure 4.1 Watermarking Process.

like pictures or videos. They often appear in television broadcasting or stock photos. They are often found in stock photos or during television broadcasting [4]. On the other hand, invisible watermarks are integrated in such a way that they do not affect the visual quality of the material and are only identified through specific algorithms. These are usually employed for copyright protection, verification, and forensic tracking [5].

Another way to classify the watermark is by its durability. Strong watermarks are designed to face malicious tasks such as specific signal processing tasks, compression, filtering, and cropping. This type of watermark plays an important role in areas such as copyright protection and monitoring material distribution. Delicate watermarks are extremely sensitive to any change in host media and are mainly used to identify tampering or unauthorized amendments. Even slight changes can be made to the watermark, indicating possible violations of integrity. Semi-fragile watermarks act as an agreement, which allows some harmless adjustments, such as harmful compression, while still being capable of deliberate, intentional tampering [6].

In addition, the watermark can also be divided into static and dynamic types. All copies of static watermark media are uniform, while dynamic watermarks differ for each user or delivery example, causing them to be particularly effective for hiking and fingerprinting. Dynamic watermarking is beneficial in conditions such as pay-per-view or digital content licensing, where it is important to find out the leaked copy.

4.3 Classification of Watermarking Techniques

Digital-watermarking techniques can be classified based on various criteria, such as the domain where the watermark is inserted, its visibility, the necessary strength level, and its intended use. One of the most prevalent classifications is defined by the embedding domain, which includes spatial- and transform-domain techniques. In spatial-domain methods, the watermark is embedded directly by changing the pixel values of the original image. These methods are directly and computationally efficient, yet they are less flexible against specific image-processing tasks, including compression or filtering. A well-known example of such techniques is the LSB method [7].

Figure 4.2 depicts various types of watermarking techniques, categorized based on the type of cover file. In text watermarking, the cover file can be in the form of text documents, Portable Document Formats (PDFs), or Word files. Its primary applications include preventing plagiarism, ensuring authentication, and maintaining document integrity. In image watermarking, the cover file may consist of formats such as JPEG, Tagged Image File Format (TIFF), Bit Map Pixel (BMP), or Portable Network Graphics (PNG). This technique is commonly applied to protect confidential documents, enforce copyright, and verify authenticity. In audio watermarking, the hidden information is embedded within audio signals like WAV, MP3, or AAC files. It is mainly used for securing music tracks, broadcast monitoring, and detecting unauthorized copies. As the name suggests, video watermarking uses video files as cover media. It plays a vital role in protecting digital rights, verifying authenticity, and tracking piracy.

In blind watermarking, the retrieval of the hidden watermark does not require the original cover file. Only the watermark itself is needed for detection. This method is widely applied in copyright protection of multimedia files and in broadcast monitoring. For example, a watermark can be extracted from an image without the need for its original uncompressed version.

In semi-blind watermarking, partial information, such as the watermark pattern or a secret key, is required for extraction, but not the

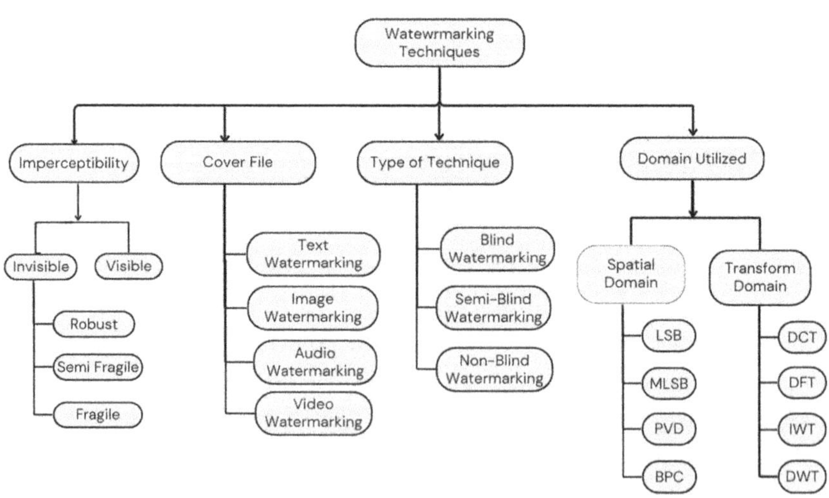

Figure 4.2 Watermarking Techniques.

original cover file. It relies on auxiliary information and involves some computational complexity, which enhances the robustness of the watermark. Its key applications include ownership verification, where the detector can compare the extracted watermark with the original for quality validation.

In fragile watermarking, even small modifications to the cover file can distort or destroy the watermark. Due to this sensitivity, it cannot withstand compression or common signal-processing attacks. However, this very property makes it highly useful for tamper detection and document integrity verification.

Watermarking can be either visible or invisible. This work focuses on the domain in which the secret information is embedded. The spatial and transform domains are further classified into methods such as LSB, MSB, PVD, DWT, Integer Wavelet Transform (IWT), DCT, and others. Watermarking techniques in spatial domains include directly changing the pixel values of a digital image to embed the watermark. These approaches are usually simple, quick, and efficient, making them suitable for real-time or low-resource scenarios. A commonly used method in this group is LSB replacement, which replaces the least important bits of the selected pixel with watermark information. Since the adjustment of these bits has a minimal effect on the image quality, LSB is known for its high indispensability. However, it is especially susceptible to general attacks, such as compression, noise introduction, and cropping, which can easily compromise or change embedded watermarks [8].

Other spatial-domain methods include patchwork algorithms that use statistical techniques to accommodate the random pairs of pixels based on a Gaussian distribution to embed the watermark. Although they can be stronger than LSB, they still have limited resistance to geometric modifications or filtering. Another spatial-domain technique is the bit-plane slicing method. This technique breaks an image into its bit planes and inserts the watermark into a specific plane, often one of the middle-order planes, to maintain a balance between visibility and durability [9]. Unlike LSB techniques, the methods of bit plane can give a slightly better strengthening by navigation at least important layers, although they are also unsafe for processing attacks. Spatial-domain watermarking is beneficial due to its speed and simplicity.

In MSB watermarking, the watermark is embedded into the most significant bits of the cover file. This technique often results in visible watermarking and is generally robust against various attacks. However, it may cause slight degradation in the quality of the cover file. The capacity of MSB watermarking is relatively low, as data are embedded in the bits that have the greatest impact on the original content. This method works by replacing the most significant bits of the cover file with the corresponding bits from the watermark.

In PVD watermarking, the difference between neighboring pixels in an image is calculated to embed the secret message as represented in Figure 4.3. A larger difference between two adjacent pixels allows more data to be hidden without increasing the risk of detection. Conversely, a smaller difference means less data can be embedded to avoid being noticed by the human eye. This technique leverages the fact that the human visual system is less sensitive to changes in high-contrast (edge) areas than in low-contrast regions. As a result, PVD causes minimal visible distortion to the cover image. Although it is more complex than LSB-based methods, it offers enhanced security for the embedded watermark.

Bit-Plane Complexity (BPC) watermarking is a technique that hides the watermark by analyzing the complexity of individual bit-planes in the cover image. Bit-planes represent the image data at different bit levels. Bit-planes with higher complexity can conceal more data compared to those with lower complexity. Since changes in complex regions are less noticeable to the human eye, this method maintains high visual quality of the watermarked image. It offers moderate data-hiding capacity and is well-suited for embedding

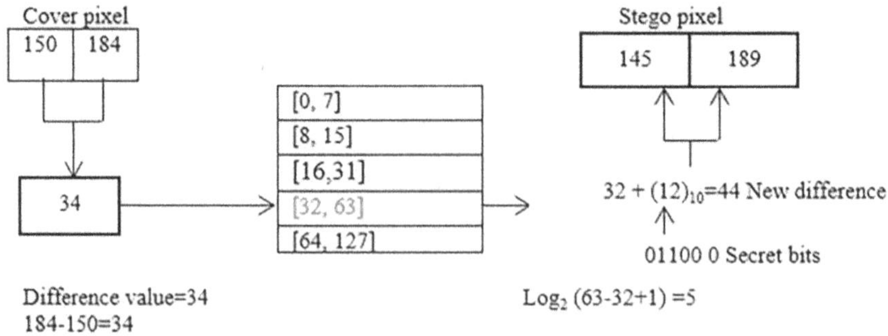

Figure 4.3 PVD Watermarking Process.

information selectively. Although it is more complex than LSB and MSB watermarking, it effectively balances imperceptibility, robustness, and embedding capacity.

The DCT facilitates an ingenious means of concealing crucial intelligence, for instance, copyright notices or verification particulars, within electronic illustrations in a fashion that is barely perceptible to human visual perception and withstands prevalent image handling practices. In this specialized technique, the host illustration is originally sectioned into minuscule squares, traditionally spanning 8x8 pixels, and DCT is applied to every square to translate pixel valuations from real geographic coordinates into the frequency domain, where the information can be hidden in the diagram's DCT coefficients. While a capable strategy, solely the most adroit coders can properly insert and later decrypt the concealed data, distinguishing authorized content and its origins [10].

During extraction, the same DCT process is used to retrieve the watermark from the altered coefficients, allowing identification of copyrighted content despite alterations from compression or other transformations relying on the DCT. For assessment, techniques like PSNR, MSE, and concealing capacity can provide quantification of a watermarking method's robustness against interference while maintaining imperceptibility, which is critical for applications in copyright protection and verification of multimedia. The DCT, central to both watermark embedding and techniques including lossy formats like JPEG that might attempt removal of embedded signatures, makes such spatial-domain techniques well-suited to confirming authenticity even after various processes alter the signal [11].

The DWT watermarking technique is a widely utilized approach in digital image watermarking that capitalizes on the multi-level examination ability of wavelets. In this strategy, the cover image is separated into diverse frequency sub bands—usually LL, LH, HL, and HH—using DWT. The watermark is inserted into one or more of these sub-bands; frequently, the LL or mid-frequency zones are opted for to guarantee a balance between resilience and imperceptibility. Moreover, the watermark can be hidden across sub-bands or inside the coefficients of a single sub-band, relying on the desired properties. The selection of sub-bands and coefficients impacts the strength of the embedded watermark against anticipated attacks [12]. The working of

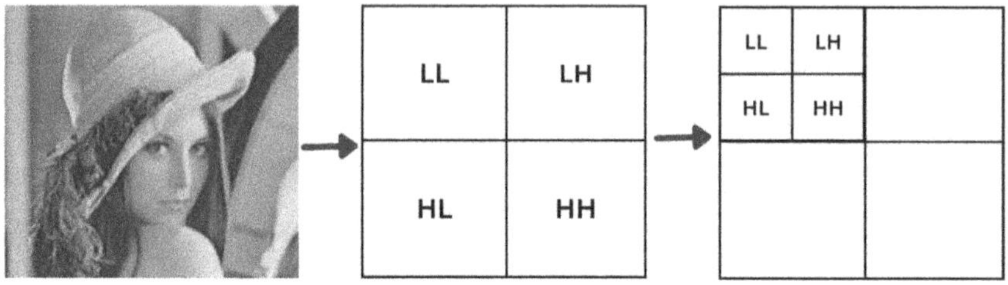

Figure 4.4 DWT Watermarking Process.

the DWT technique is shown in Figure 4.4, which shows how blocks are divided to hide the secret message in high-frequency components.

While manipulating wavelet coefficients instead of pixel values allows for DWT watermarking, withstanding numerous image-handling techniques such as compression, filtering, and noise introduction, directly editing wavelet coefficients, then applying the inverse DWT for reconstruction of the watermarked image, remains a favored approach. This methodology exploits the DWT's capacity for spatial and frequency data localization, crafting an effective solution for applications demanding robust, enduring watermarks to provide digital rights administration and image validation. Despite compressing, sharpening, or adding interference to a watermarked image, the covert tag continues untouched, fortified by the DWT's separation of an image's analytic constituents [13].

Table 4.1 illustrates the differences between various watermarking techniques. The comparison is based on parameters such as embedding domain, type of cover file, robustness, visual quality, and typical use cases. Each technique has its own advantages and limitations. The level of security depends largely on the amount of secret data embedded. The effectiveness of a watermarking method is evaluated by factors including the quality of the stego file, hiding capacity, and resilience against attacks. Achieving a balance among these parameters is essential for developing an efficient and reliable watermarking technique.

4.4 Challenges in Watermarking

Some of the watermarking challenges are listed as follows in Figure 4.5 [14, 15]:

Table 4.1 Differences between Watermarking Methods

PARAMETERS	SPATIAL DOMAIN	FREQUENCY DOMAIN	VISIBLE WATERMARKING	INVISIBLE WATERMARKING	ROBUST WATERMARKING	FRAGILE WATERMARKING
Concealing Process	Directly, pixels are modified	Utilize the frequency domain to conceal data	Watermark is visible	Watermark is concealed in the cover file	It conceals secret data in such a way that the concealed data is robust against attacks.	Breaks with minor updates
Stego Visual Quality	Stego is sometimes of poor quality	Stego visual quality is high	It is visible to human eyes	It is imperceptible	Stego visual quality is high, so robust against attacks	Imperceptible until altered
Robustness	It is simple to implement, so not so robust	It is difficult to implement so robustly against attacks	Watermark is visible	Robustness varies with the technique used	High	Medium
Computational Complexity	It is simple	It takes time to hide data	It is simple and easy	Its complexity varies	It is difficult to implement and requires more resources and time	Complexity varies depending on the technique used to hide data
Uses	Image watermarking is one of the major application	Copyright protection, authentication of data	Ownership display, branding	Copyright, authentication of data	Copyright protection, forensic tracking	Tamper detection and authentication of data
Compression attack	Secret data is detected in a compression attack	It is not detectable when applying compression	It has been preserved many times	On concealing a large amount of data may be detectable	It is robust against compression	It is detectable on compression

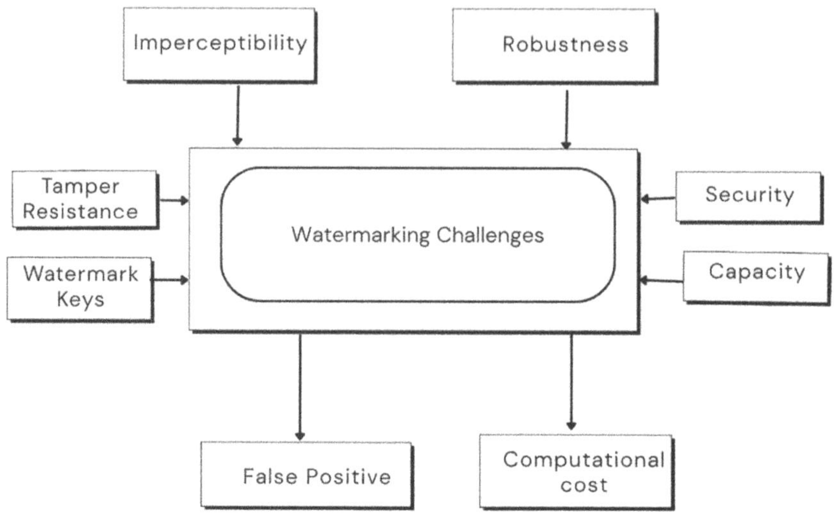

Figure 4.5 Watermarking Challenges.

- Watermarking methods must be exported in one or more areas to balance the size of the payload, the invisibility of the watermark, and its flexibility for attacks.
- Specific actions such as JPEG or Moving Picture Expert Group (MPEG) compression, filtering, noise connecting, and shaping can compromise embedded watermarks.
- Once the embedding algorithm is detected, anti-assessment, or removal methods can be used to detect the presence of fake watermarks.
- Processes such as rotation, scaling, translation, and cropping can incorrectly identify or remove the watermark completely.
- Inconsistent testing standards and datasets have made it challenging to make a proper comparison of various watermarking techniques and impartially compare them.
- To avoid watermark change or illegal removal, embedding and extraction keys must be protected from unwanted access.
- In sensitive areas such as medical imaging or legal documentation, reversible watermarking should ensure innocent recovery of original materials, which adds to complexity.

- Advanced or hybrid methods (such as DWT–DCT or deep learning) usually require adequate processing power and memory, which can restrict their use in real-time or resource-limited settings.

4.5 Emerging Trends and Future Directions

Some of the trends and future direction are suggested below [16, 17]:

Deep Learning-Based Watermarking: Use of deep learning methods for strong watermark embedding and extraction.
Quantum Watermarking: Taking advantage of quantum properties for theoretically unbreakable watermarking.
Blockchain Integration: Irreversible record-keeping for watermark certification.
Reverse Watermarking: Important for medical and legal fields, where original data recovery must be possible.
Network Watermarking: Hiding data in the header and traffic is safer than normal steganography.
3D Watermarking: Concealing secret data in 3D files has more options than the 2D cover files.

4.6 Conclusion

In a rapidly digital world, digital watermarking is becoming an important technique to protect multimedia content. This review has analyzed various watermarking methods, classified according to the application, strength, visibility of the watermark, and the domain. The spatial domain-based techniques are known for their ease of use and computational effectiveness. Transform-domain techniques such as DCT, DWT, and a hybrid approach are more favorable for the flexibility and high security applications. In addition, new techniques such as blockchain, quantum computing, and machine learning can be included to make even more flexible and safe watermarking options to proceed as watermarking methods. The importance of watermarking will only increase to protect intellectual property, guarantee authenticity, and make material tracking and monitoring easier because multimedia material takes the center stage in the digital environment.

References

[1] Begum, M., & Uddin, M. S. (2020). Digital image watermarking techniques: A review. *Information*, *11*(2), 110.

[2] Kadian, P., Arora, S. M., & Arora, N. (2021). Robust digital watermarking techniques for copyright protection of digital data: A survey. *Wireless Personal Communications*, *118*, 3225–3249.

[3] Singh, H. K., & Singh, A. K. (2023). Comprehensive review of watermarking techniques in deep-learning environments. *Journal of Electronic Imaging*, *32*(3), 031804–031804.

[4] Ghrare, S. E., Alamari, A. A. M., & Emhemed, H. A. (2022, May). Digital image watermarking method based on LSB and DWT hybrid technique. In *2022, IEEE 2nd International Maghreb Meeting of the Conference on Sciences and Techniques of Automatic Control and Computer Engineering (MI-STA)* (pp. 465–470). IEEE.

[5] Alarood, A. A. (2022). Improve the efficiency for embedding in LSB method based digital image watermarking. *Journal of Theoretical and Applied Information Technology*, *100*(15), 1–15.

[6] Arulananth, T. S., Jayanthi, S., Kiran, P. S., Chinnasamy, P., Kavitha, S., & Saravanan, K. (2025). Secured certificate generation using LSB and hybrid watermarking using MATLAB. In *Integrated Technologies in Electrical, Electronics and Biotechnology Engineering* (pp. 54–59). CRC Press.

[7] Kumar, S., & Singh, B. K. (2021). DWT based color image watermarking using maximum entropy. *Multimedia Tools and Applications*, *80*, 15487–15510.

[8] Radha Kumari, R., Vijaya Kumar, V., & Rama Naidu, K. (2024). Deep learning-based image watermarking technique with hybrid DWT-SVD. *The Imaging Science Journal*, *72*(6), 749–765.

[9] Fares, K., Khaldi, A., Redouane, K., & Salah, E. (2021). DCT & DWT based watermarking scheme for medical information security. *Biomedical Signal Processing and Control*, *66*, 102403.

[10] Laxmanika, & Singh, P. K. (2022). Robust and imperceptible image watermarking technique based on SVD, DCT, BEMD and PSO in wavelet domain. *Multimedia Tools and Applications*, *81*(16), 22001–22026.

[11] Zhu, T., Qu, W., & Cao, W. (2022). An optimized image watermarking algorithm based on SVD and IWT. *The Journal of Supercomputing*, *78*(1), 222–237.

[12] Meng, L., Liu, L., Tian, G., & Wang, X. (2021). An adaptive reversible watermarking in IWT domain. *Multimedia Tools and Applications*, *80*, 711–735.

[13] Singh, B., & Kasana, G. (2024, November). A review of digital watermarking techniques: Current trends, challenges and opportunities. In *Web Intelligence* (Vol. 22, No. 4, pp. 523–553). SAGE Publications.

[14] Dubey, A., Dixit, N., Arora, R., Mishra, J., Shrivastava, D. D., & Kinger, S. (2024, August). Challenges and opportunities in digital image watermarking. In *2024 First International Conference on Pioneering Developments in Computer Science & Digital Technologies (IC2SDT)* (pp. 29–34). IEEE.

[15] Singh, R., Saraswat, M., Ashok, A., Mittal, H., Tripathi, A., Pandey, A. C., & Pal, R. (2023). From classical to soft computing based watermarking techniques: A comprehensive review. *Future Generation Computer Systems*, *141*, 738–754.

[16] Pilania, U., Kumar, M., & Mittal, V. (2023). Performance evaluation of LSB steganography based on multiple image formats. *Journal of Discrete Mathematical Sciences and Cryptography*, *26*(7), 1911–1924.

[17] Pilania, U., Kumar, M., & Kaur, G. (2022, February). Region of interest using viola-jones algorithm for video steganography. In *International Conference on Computing in Engineering & Technology* (pp. 405–415). Springer Nature Singapore.

5

Video Steganography

Techniques, Challenges, and Future Trends

5.1 Introduction

In today's digital era, the web is widely used for transmitting all types of information, including confidential data. Ensuring the security of such sensitive information is of paramount importance. However, with advancements in technology and the increasing expertise of malicious users, the threat of hacking has grown significantly. To safeguard secret information, more sophisticated protection techniques are required. Among these, steganography plays a vital role. Traditionally, cryptography has been employed to secure information by converting it into an unintelligible form, thereby preventing unauthorized individuals from understanding it [1]. In contrast, steganography takes a different approach by concealing the very existence of secret information within a cover medium, making it less likely to attract attention.

Steganography techniques can be categorized based on the type of cover file used, namely text, image, audio, and video steganography. Text steganography generally offers low hiding capacity, and when large secret messages are embedded, they can be easily detected through image processing or statistical attacks. Image steganography, on the other hand, provides a higher concealing capacity due to the relatively larger size of image files. Since images are widely shared across the web, this method has become particularly popular among researchers. Video steganography involves embedding information within video files, offering greater flexibility and capacity because of their dynamic content and large file size [2].

Figure 5.1 illustrates the flow of the steganography process between sender and receiver, where a video file is used as the cover medium

DOI: 10.1201/9781003504139-5

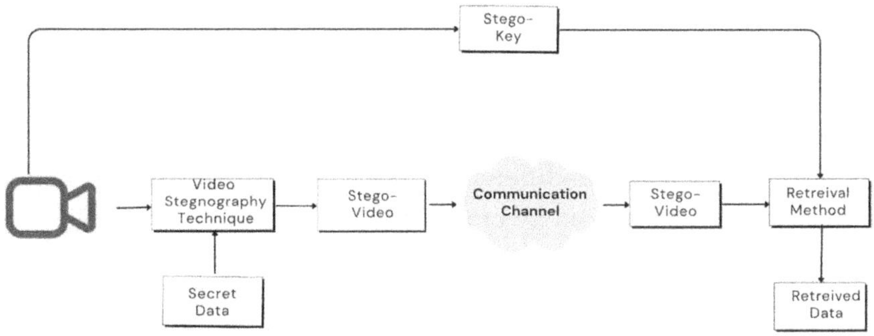

Figure 5.1 Video steganography process.

and the secret data are in the form of an image. To enhance security, a secret key may also be employed; however, this increases computational complexity. In the embedding phase, the video is divided into multiple frames, and one or more frames are selected to conceal the secret information. The frame containing the hidden data is referred to as a stego frame. At the receiver's end, the reverse process is carried out to extract the hidden information from the stego file.

This review presents a comprehensive analysis of current video steganography techniques. It classifies and compares existing methods based on their primary mechanism within spatial, frequency, and compressed domains. Additionally, it examines state-of-the-art progress that integrates the approach to deep learning and machine learning. Primary assessment criteria include payload capacity, strengthening against attacks, and resistance to steganalysis, which are examined with frequent challenges in the region. Analyzing each approach's strengths and boundaries highlights the trends that discussed this chapter and provides a holistic view of the position of video steganography. The systematic review contributes valuable insight into the current and future communication scenario hidden through digital video media.

5.2 Video Steganography Techniques

Video steganography techniques are mainly classified based on the data embedding domain. The three main domains include spatial domains, transform domains, and compressed domains. In spatial-domain methods, secret information is embedded by directly revising the pixel values within the video frame. One of this category's most commonly used techniques is LSB replacement, where the least significant bits of pixel values are replaced with bits from hidden messages. Another method, PVD, uses the difference between adjacent pixels to determine how much data can be embedded with greater pixel differences for high embedding capacity [3]. Some of the video steganography techniques are shown in Figure 5.2. The significant difference between the spatial domain, transform domain, and compression techniques is provided in Table 5.1.

Spatial-domain techniques are computationally efficient and straightforward in hiding secret messages. Because changes made in pixel values are often minimal, they are incorporated by the human eye. However, these methods are highly unsafe for common image and video processing operations, such as compression, filtering, and resizing, which can easily distort or destroy embedded data [4].

Regarding video steganography, the PVD is operated by analyzing the brightness variation between the adjacent pixels within the video frame. The central concept of hiding a secret message is that significant intensity differences are usually found with edges in an image, where the human visual system is less sensitive to minor changes. More data can be embedded in these edge areas without noticeable visual deformation. Conversely, less data are hidden in smooth areas with slight pixel differences to avoid detection. This adaptive strategy

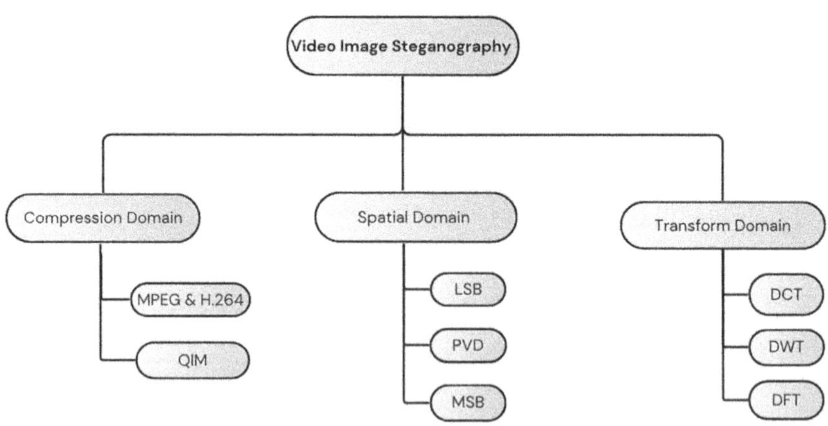

Figure 5.2 Video steganography types.

Table 5.1 Video Steganography Techniques Difference

ASPECT	SPATIAL DOMAIN STEGANOGRAPHY	TRANSFORM DOMAIN STEGANOGRAPHY	COMPRESSION STEGANOGRAPHY
Concealing Secret Message	The secret message is hidden in pixel intensity values	The secret message is hidden in the frequency coefficients	The secret message is hidden during the compression process
Most Commonly Used Techniques	LSB substitution, PVD	DCT for middle-frequency concealing, DWT sub-band concealing	JPEG compression, Huffman code alteration
Complexity Level	Simple and easy to hide secret message	It's tricky to hide a secret message, so it's more robust against attacks.	Embedding complexity varies from method to method
Robustness	Detectable against some image-processing attacks	More robust to many image-processing attacks compared to spatial-domain techniques	Robustness depends on the compression format
Visual Quality	When hiding a large amount of data, the visual quality of the stego file may degrade.	It can hide more data without degrading the visual quality of the stego file.	Visual quality is high if embedded carefully during compression
Robustness to Compression	It is less robust against compression	It is more robust against compression	Robustness depends on the format of information
Concealing Time	In it, concealing takes less time	It does slow concealing, as before concealing transformation needs to be done, and then the inverse transformation.	It takes less time compared to transform-domain techniques
Variation in File Size	File size remains the same, usually	File size remains the same, usually	Sometimes slightly increase

helps maintain visual quality by maximizing payload capacity in more tolerant regions [5].

The LSB method is one of the simplest techniques in the spatial domain [6]. In this approach, the least significant bits of the cover medium are substituted with the bits of the secret message. While LSB is straightforward to implement, it is also highly vulnerable, as the hidden data can be easily detected by attackers. Moreover, it lacks robustness against common image-processing operations and steganalysis attacks. Despite these limitations, LSB can be applied across various forms of steganography, including text, image, audio, and video. In contrast, transform-domain techniques offer greater robustness by converting the cover file from the spatial domain into the frequency or time domain before embedding the secret message [7].

In the DCT technique, images are devided into blocks and then convert into frequency components. The secret data is hidden in the mid-frequency components. Low frequencies are left unchanged to preserve image quality, while high frequencies are avoided due to their sensitivity to compression. Since DCT is widely used in video compression standards such as MPEG and JPEG, embedding allows for efficient integration during the compression process. Although it is more complex than spatial methods, DCT steganography is robust and preferred for the secure information exchange [8].

DWT-based steganography uses wavelet transforms to break a video frame into several sub-bands at various resolution levels. These include LL, LH, HL, and HH bands. Secret information is usually hidden in high sub-bands like (LH, HL, HH), which represent fine image details like the edges. This allows for suitable data hiding because changes in these areas are less noticeable. DWT provides both spatial and frequency information, making it more optimal. These everyday video processing operations, such as compression, scaling, and exteriors, produce better crops. While DWT is computationally more intensive, it is favored in high-protection applications where attacks require strong hidden and resistance [9].

DFT-based steganography converts the frame into the frequency domain using the Fourier transform. This method breaks the video into sinusoidal components, organizing the data into the low-, medium-, and high-frequency bands. Secret information is usually hidden by changing the magnitude or phase of the Fourier coefficient. Since the human eye is less sensitive to small changes in these qualities, this approach provides high indispensability. A significant strength of DFT steganography is its flexibility for geometric changes, such as rotation and scaling, which usually affect spatial-domain methods. However, DFT is more complex and computationally demanding. Nevertheless, it provides better security and is ideal for applications where privacy and strength are essential [10].

Compressed-domain steganography directly compresses video frames, including embedding secret data, which uses video coding standards such as MPEG and H.264. These methods eliminate the requirement of complete disruption in the cover file, making them efficient for real-time applications. However, they are highly dependent on the composition and behavior of specific codes, which can introduce challenges related to adaptability and strength in various compression settings. This domain has a common approach speed vector modification. Motion vectors, which describe the movement of blocks between video frames for inter-frame compression, can change the secret information slightly to encoded secret information without affecting the video quality. These features of compression steganography make it a practical and secret method [11].

Another widely used technique is the Permutation Index Modulation (PIM), which embeds the data during compression in the quantity of DCT coefficients. The flow of data concealing and retrieval is shown in Figures 5.3 and 5.4, respectively. Since these coefficients are the main ones for compressed video content representation, replacing them carefully allows them to preserve visual allegiance to safe embedding [12]. More advanced techniques include embedding data into the macroblock header or entropy coding structures. These methods insert the information hidden in some parts of the video bitstream that are not directly related to visual quality, offering high hiding and strength. For example, the entropy coding of the symbol in the variable-length code (e.g., Huffman or arithmetic coding) modifies the mapping, which selects between equivalent representatives for secret encoding. This allows for intensive integration in the compression pipeline with minimal risk of detection – but the video stream requires accuracy to avoid corruption [13].

Another powerful method is residual data embedding. The difference between the estimated and actual frames is stored as residual data in predictive video coding (as used in MPEG and H.264). These

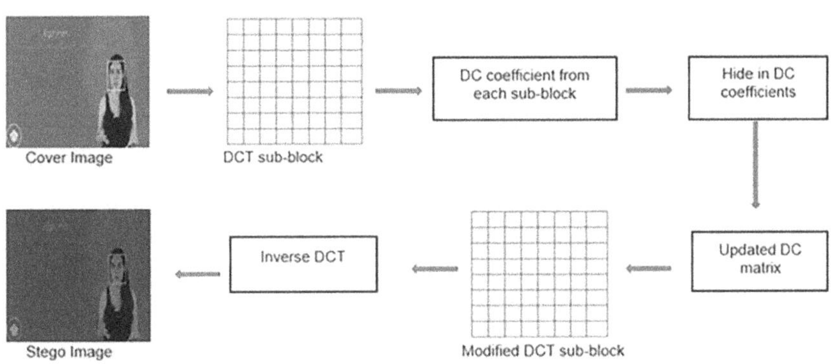

Figure 5.3 DCT concealing process [20].

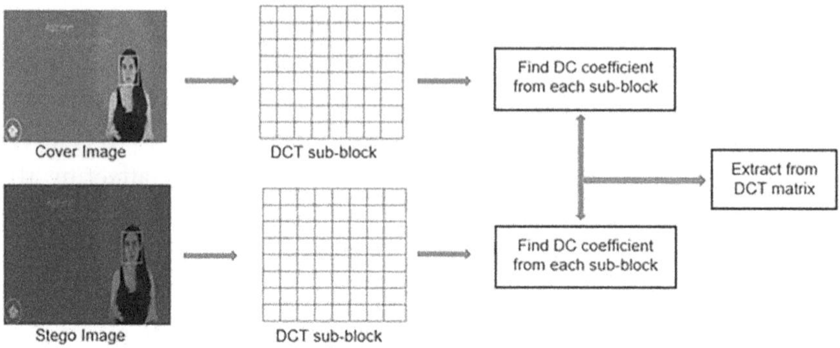

Figure 5.4 DCT retrieval process [20].

remains contain precise knowledge and are less sensitive to compression artifacts, making them ideal for hiding data. By slightly modifying the cover file, secret information can be re-encoded with a large amount of secret data, and provide flexibility. The compressed-domain technique offers substantial benefits in strength, safety, and integration with real-world video systems. However, these methods require compression standards and intensive knowledge of accurate implementation to maintain video integrity. When handled correctly, these methods provide effective communication for applications such as secure video transmission, secret monitoring, and high-protection data embedding [14, 15].

5.3 Challenges in Video Steganography

Some of the existing challenges are listed and also shown in Figure 5.5 as well [16, 17]:

- Spatial-domain techniques are simple and easy to hide the secret data, so these techniques are sensitive to image-processing attacks.
- These techniques have low embedding capacity. When embedding a large amount of data, the visual quality degrades.
- Transform-domain techniques are robust but require computational effort and time.
- When a large amount of data is concealed, the visual quality of the stego file may degrade.

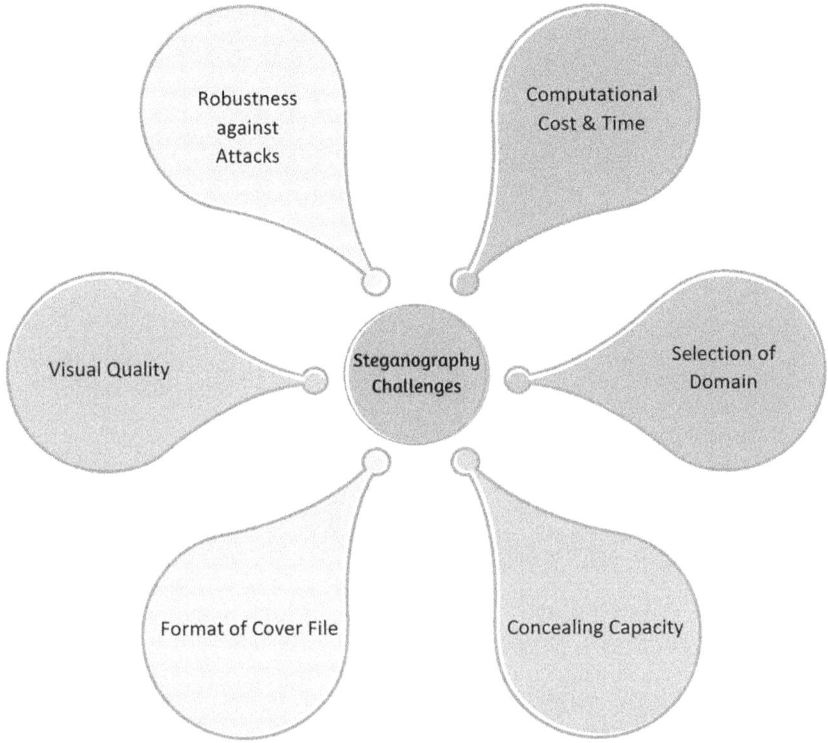

Figure 5.5 Challenges in steganography.

- There is a trade-off between the concealing capacity, imperceptibility, and robustness. On increasing any one parameter, the other two were affected.
- In compression techniques, compression capacity may drop due to hiding a large amount of data.
- Some techniques cannot work on all the cover and secret file formats.
- In compression techniques, compatibility issues may arise.

5.4 Future Trends

Some of the future trends for spatial-domain, transform-domain, and compression steganography techniques are listed as shown in Figure 5.6 as well [18, 19]:

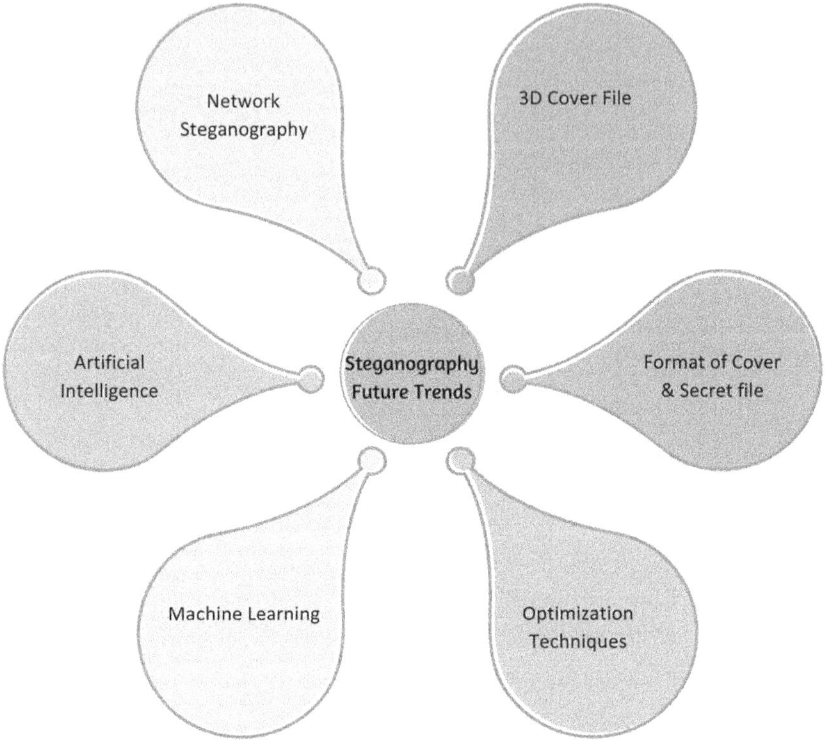

Figure 5.6 Steganography future trends.

- Adaptive pixel modification can be done to improve image quality depending on the texture of input images.
- AI and ML techniques can be applied to find where secret data can be concealed.
- The use of artificial techniques helps in avoiding image-processing attacks.
- Machine learning techniques can find a more suitable frequency coefficient where secret data may be concealed.
- Optimization techniques help compress the data to hide more information in the cover file.
- 3D cover files can be utilized to increase the concealing capacity.
- Network steganography techniques are considered more secure and efficient for concealing secret data in protocols and traffic.

5.5 Conclusion

Finally, video steganography has become an essential tool for safe and secret communication in the digital age, which offers diverse techniques to embed information within video content. This review has examined several approaches, including spatial-domain methods such as LSB and PVD, and more refined frequency-domain techniques such as DCT, DFT, and DWT. Additionally, compression-based methods have increased the practicality and flexibility of steganography in real-world applications. Each technique presents its own trade-offs regarding embedding capacity, visual irreversibility, and resistance to detection or deformation. The progress in computing power and algorithm design continues to improve video steganography solutions' performance, safety, and adaptability.

References

[1] Valandar, M. Y., Ayubi, P., Barani, M. J., & Irani, B. Y. (2022). A chaotic video steganography technique for carrying different types of secret messages. *Journal of information security and applications, 66*, 103160.

[2] Selim, N. M., Guirguis, S. K., & Hassan, Y. F. (2022). Video steganography for image and text using deep genetic algorithm and LSB. *International Journal of Network Security, 24*(1), 140–146.

[3] Jebur, S. A., Nawar, A. K., Kadhim, L. E., & Jahefer, M. M. (2023). Hiding information in digital images using LSB steganography technique. *International Journal of Interactive Mobile Technologies, 17*(7), 167–178.

[4] Sahib, H. G. A. U. L., & Khodher, M. A. A. A. (2021). Comparison of three proposal methods in steganography encryption secret message using PVD and MapReduce. *Iraqi Journal of Computers, Communications, Control & Systems Engineering, 21*(2), 2021.

[5] Pilania, U., & Gupta, P. (2020). Analysis and implementation of IWT-SVD scheme for video steganography. In *Micro-Electronics and Telecommunication Engineering: Proceedings of 3rd ICMETE 2019* (pp. 153–162). Springer Singapore.

[6] Siddiqui, T. J., & Khare, A. (2021). Chaos-based video steganography method in discrete cosine transform domain. *International Journal of Image and Graphics, 21*(02), 2150015.

[7] Gnanitha, G., Swetha, A., Sai Teja, G., Sri Vasavi, D., & Lakshmi Sirisha, B. (2022, November). Review on image steganography transform domain techniques. In *Conference of Innovative Product Design and Intelligent Manufacturing System* (pp. 501–512). Springer Nature Singapore.

[8] Patel, R., Lad, K., Patel, M., & Desai, M. (2021). An efficient DCT-SBPM based video steganography in compressed domain. *International Journal of Information Technology*, *13*, 1073–1078.
[9] Dalal, M., & Juneja, M. (2022). A secure video steganography scheme using DWT based on object tracking. *Information Security Journal: A Global Perspective*, *31*(2), 196–213.
[10] Pilania, U., Tanwar, R., & Gupta, P. (2022). An ROI-based robust video steganography technique using SVD in wavelet domain. *Open Computer Science*, *12*(1), 1–16.
[11] Pilania, U., Tanwar, R., Zamani, M., & Manaf, A. A. (2022). Framework for video steganography using integer wavelet transform and JPEG compression. *Future Internet*, *14*(9), 254.
[12] Modupe, A. O., Adedoyin, A. E., Titilayo, A. O., & Deborah, F. O. (2021). A comparative analysis of LSB, MSB and PVD based image steganography. *International Journal of Research and Review*, *8*(9), 373–377.
[13] Suresh, M., & Shatheesh Sam, I. (2021). A secure video steganography using framelet transform and singular value decomposition. In *Data Intelligence and Cognitive Informatics: Proceedings of ICDICI 2020* (pp. 781–790). Springer Singapore.
[14] Mou, C., Xu, Y., Song, J., Zhao, C., Ghanem, B., & Zhang, J. (2023). Large-capacity and flexible video steganography via invertible neural network. In *Proceedings of the IEEE/CVF Conference on Computer Vision and Pattern Recognition* (pp. 22606–22615).
[15] Pilania, U., Tanwar, R., & Gupta, P. (2021). Stable high capacity video steganography in wavelet domain. *Turkish Journal of Computer and Mathematics Education*, *12*(7), 2142–2158.
[16] Pilania, U., Kumar, M., Rohit, T., & Nandal, N. (2023). A walk-through towards network steganography techniques. *Informatics and Automation*, *22*(5), 1103–1151.
[17] Tanwar, R., Pilania, U., Zamani, M., & Manaf, A. A. (2021). An analysis of 3D steganography techniques. *Electronics*, *10*(19), 2357.
[18] Pilania, U., Kumar, M., & Mittal, V. (2023). Performance evaluation of LSB steganography based on multiple image formats. *Journal of Discrete Mathematical Sciences and Cryptography*, *26*(7), 1911–1924.
[19] Pilania, U., Tanwar, R., Zamani, M., & Manaf, A. A. (2022). Framework for video steganography using integer wavelet transform and JPEG compression. *Future Internet*, *14*(9), 254.
[20] Pilania, U., Tanwar, R., & Gupta, P. (2021). An optimized video steganography technique using hybrid approach, Thesis.

6

A Comprehensive Study of Steganalysis Tools

Applications and Challenges

6.1 Introduction

Stegdetect is one of the first and still best-known programs built just to detect hidden data in JPEG files. Made for UNIX systems, it tracks steganography from classic tools like JSteg, JPHide, OutGuess, and F5 by matching signatures in the file. The program checks JPEG headers and quantization tables for odd patterns left by the embedding routine. Because it works fast and can scan thousands of images in minutes, many forensics teams keep it on hand. It also fails against encrypted payloads to look exactly like normal image data. Despite its coincidences, Stegdetect still holds the spot of go-to first step for forensic pros who want a quick peek at whether a batch of JPEGs might be hiding stego data [1].

StegExpose is a free, open-source tool aimed at lossless formats such as BMP, PNG, and the sneaky LSB method that works in those files. It integrates classic methods like RS and Sample Pair checks, along with the Chi-square and primary set tests, to sniff out tiny changes left by hidden messages. Because each of those tests looks for different statistical properties, the tool can spot objects the average eye never notices. After the scan, StegExpose hands back a confidence score so analysts can flag the most promising targets without wading through every pixel. Another big plus is its ability to hide whole folders of images at once, a feature that saves hours in bulk inspections. OpenStego Analyzer is one part of the larger OpenStego toolkit, and its main job

DOI: 10.1201/9781003504139-6

Table 6.1 Summary of Steganalysis Tools [5, 6, 7]

TOOL	SUPPORTED FORMATS	TECHNIQUE USED	STRENGTHS	LIMITATIONS
Stegdetect	JPEG	Signature-based	Fast, known formats	Poor against modern tools
StegExpose	BMP, PNG	Statistical analysis	Good detection accuracy	Limited to spatial LSB
OpenStego Analyzer	PNG, BMP	Basic pattern check	Simple, user-friendly	Not robust against advanced methods
StegSecret	Multiple	Modular detection	GUI support, flexible	Limited adaptability
DeepSteg	JPEG, PNG	Deep learning	High accuracy, adaptive	High resource requirements

is to find and check hidden messages that were added with that same program. It works only with BMP and PNG images [2].

StegSecret is a Java-based steganalysis tool designed to detect hidden data in digital images, audio, and text files created using various steganographic methods. StegSecret handles multiple image and audio formats, spotting hidden data added by popular programs like JPHide, OutGuess, and Steghide [3]. It comes with a desktop interface. By contrast, newer platforms like DeepSteg lean on deep learning-CNNs, particularly angular software that learns from vast image datasets and usually spots hidden messages with impressive speed and accuracy. DeepSteg works very differently from the classic rule-based detectors; rather than relying on manually coded signs, it studies countless clean and secretly altered images, learns their usual patterns, and determines which subtler irregularities the stego processes leave behind. By training on big batches that mix JPEGs with PNGs and every conceivable embedding method, the model grows flexible enough to spot secrets hidden in many file formats without needing a separate toolkit for each one [4]. Table 6.1 represents the summary of steganalysis tools.

6.2 Steganalysis Tools

In this chapter, the authors have worked on three steganalysis tools for detecting secret information. Many steganalysis tools have been explored based on many properties. The working of the three steganography tools has been provided as follows:

6.2.1 *Digital Invisible Ink*

This tool is designed to conceal information within various types of digital media. The hidden text remains invisible to the human eye and can only be detected using specialized tools or techniques. It is widely applied in copyright protection, authentication, and secure data transmission. The tool embeds secret data in a manner that makes it virtually undetectable. A hidden key is also employed to enhance security. The tool integrates concepts from cryptography, image processing, and steganography, and finds applications in copyright protection, intellectual property rights, official documentation, and detection of unauthorized data [8].

Figure 6.1 illustrates the tool's encoding interface. In this study, the authors consider the text to be the secret message, while an image is the cover file for concealing the text. An eight-character strong password is used to reinforce the security of the process. The text message is embedded into the image, resulting in the generation of a stego file. Figure 6.2 demonstrates the process of stego file creation. The generated stego file is preserved for later use, as it is required at the receiver's end for secret message retrieval.

Figure 6.3 illustrates the decoding process at the receiver's end. The stego file is accessed, and a password is provided to retrieve the

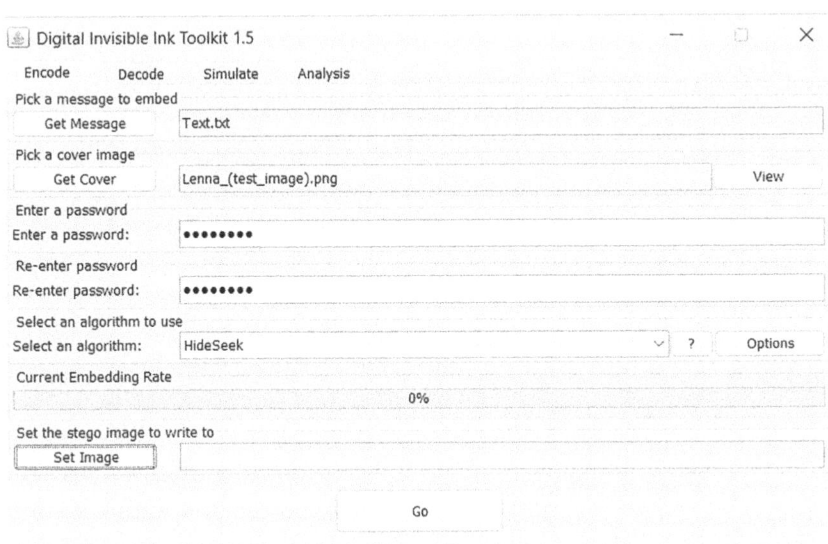

Figure 6.1 Encoding interface.

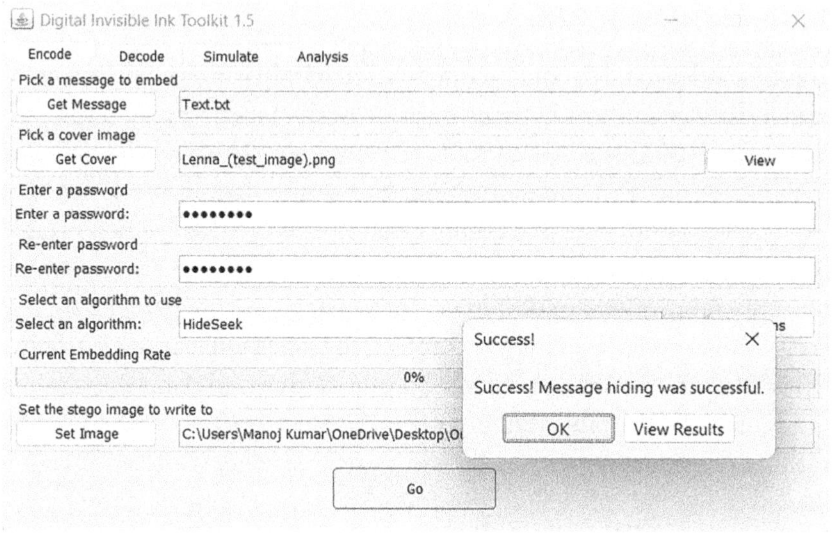

Figure 6.2 Stego image creation.

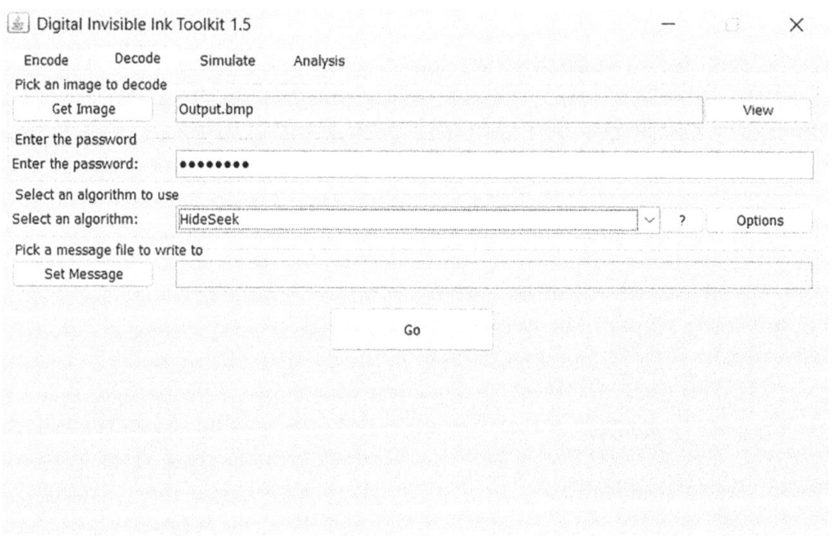

Figure 6.3 Decoding at the receiver end.

hidden message, which is obtained in text form. Figure 6.4 shows the retrieval of the secret message and its storage on the author's computer. Figure 6.5 depicts the variations in the statistical properties of the image caused by message embedding. The variations in statistical

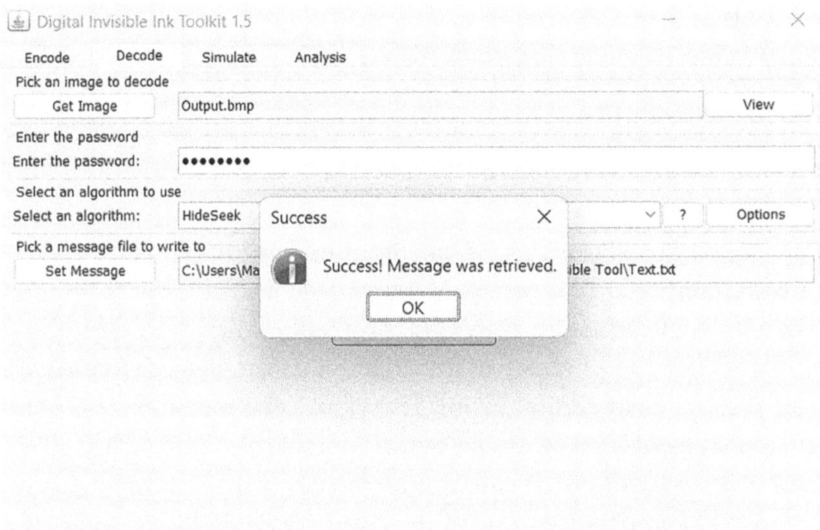

Figure 6.4 Secret message retrieved.

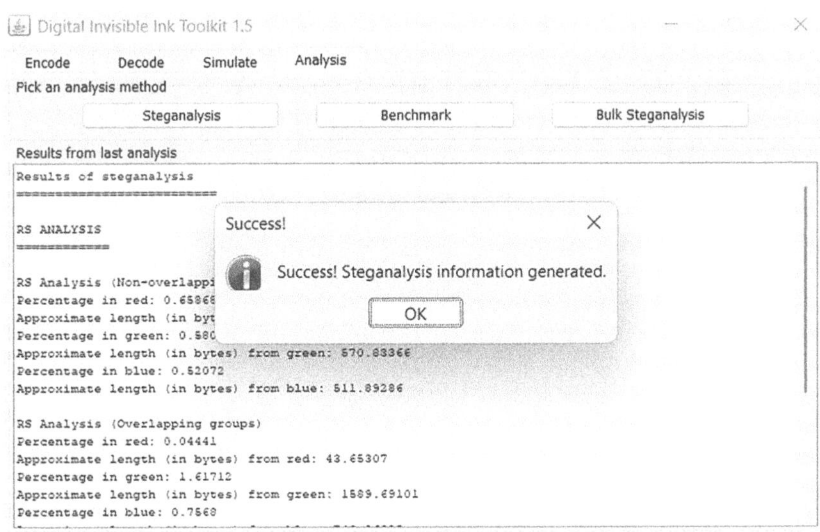

Figure 6.5 Changes in cover file properties.

properties lead to the detection of a hidden secret message. The less variation there is, the lower the chances of detecting hidden secret messages. When hiding large-sized messages, the variation in properties increases, causing low-quality stego file and, as a result, easier detection of the hidden secret message. So, there is a trade-off between hiding capacity, visual quality of the stego file, and robustness against attacks.

6.2.2 *JPEGsnoop Tool*

JPEGsnoop is a steganalysis tool that uses images and video files to embed secret data. It is an open-source tool available for Windows. It has its applications in copyright protection, digital forensics, and the authentication of sensitive information. It can detect whether the cover file has been edited or not. It explores the metadata and compression signs of images. It can detect whether the photos are edited in some software or not. It can explore the tables like Huffman, quantization, and compression facts of the cover file [9, 10].

Figure 6.6 illustrates the concealing process, where an image is used as the cover file and text is taken as the secret message. A stego file is then generated, carrying the embedded hidden message. Figure 6.7 depicts the variations in the statistical properties of the cover file, indicating that data has been concealed within it. At the receiver's end, the secret message is successfully retrieved. The weakness of the tool is that it depends on the file format. If the file format changes, detecting hidden secret messages may cause a problem. When a large amount of data is hidden, the stego quality degrades, representing a failure of the

Figure 6.6 Encoding process.

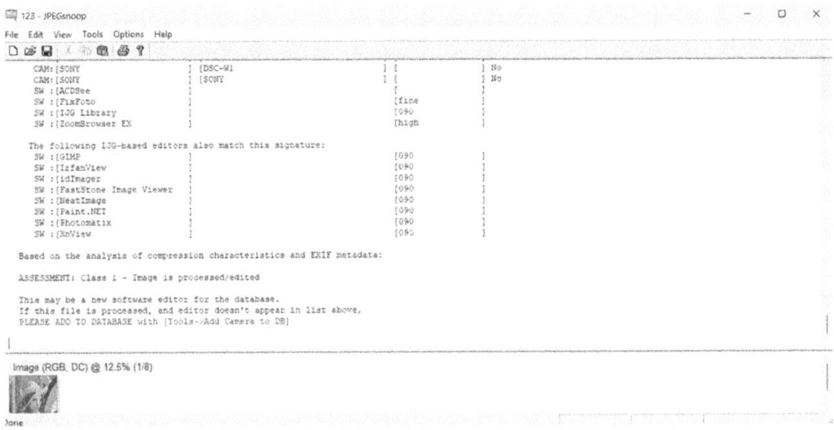

Figure 6.7 Changes in statistical properties of cover file.

steganography tool. The measure parameters in steganography are the concealing capacity, imperceptibility, and robustness. When one parameter is changed, the other two parameters are automatically affected.

6.2.3 StegDetect Tool

StegDetect is freely available for Windows. It can be downloaded for Windows as it is an open-source tool. It is efficient in detecting hidden information in cover files, and it is developed for JPEG images. It can detect hidden messages using JSteg, JPHide, OutGuess, Invisible Secrets, and many more. It has applications in forensics, law enforcement, sensitive data safety, cyber-crime, and many more [11, 12].

Figure 6.8 illustrates the embedding of a secret message into different types of cover images. The text is embedded at the sender's end, while the decoding is carried out at the receiver's. Once the secret text is embedded, the statistical properties of the cover image are altered, enabling the detection of hidden information. The detection process of the embedded secret message is shown in Figure 6.9. The tool is independent of the different file formats. It can work with all the image formats. When concealing a large amount of secret data, the tool automatically exposes the hidden secret message through the visual quality of the stego file [13].

Figure 6.8 Encoding process.

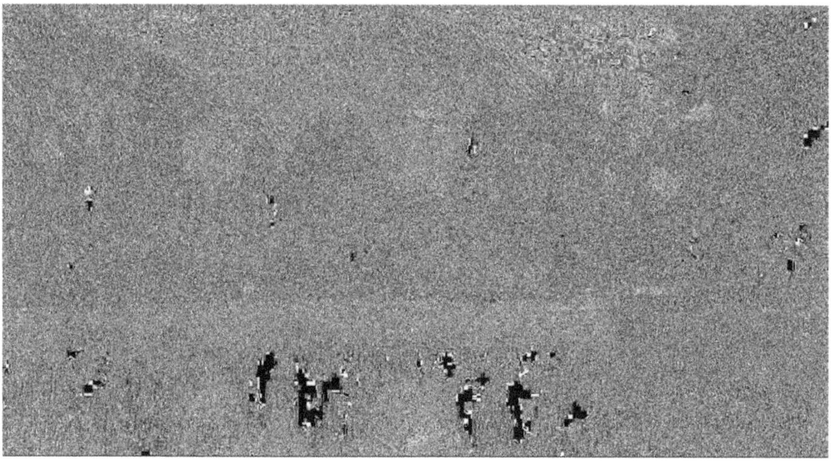

Figure 6.9 Decoding process.

6.3 Challenges in Steganalysis

Some of the challenges that still exist with steganalysis tools are listed below:

- High false positives and negatives appear when random noise turns a clean file into a false hit or when a tiny payload slips through unnoticed [14].
- Encryption and obfuscation guard hidden text behind keys; hence, even the best scanner needs a second line of defense [15].
- Format diversity keeps tools locked to narrow file types, such as JPEGs or BMPs, ignoring many documents and videos [16].
- Resource constraints force machine-learning systems to chew through power and data, slowing on-the-ground investigations [16].
- Adaptation to evasive techniques lets modern steganography use compression-aware or distortion-minimizing tricks that blur normal fingerprints [17].

6.4 Conclusion

Steganalysis protects sensitive data from unauthorized access by detecting concealed information embedded within digital media. The proposed work presents an in-depth review of various steganalysis tools and their potential applications in enhancing data security. These tools use traditional, statistical, machine-learning-based, and deep-learning-based methods to detect secret information. The study also outlines the challenges encountered during the detection of hidden data, highlighting factors that affect the robustness and effectiveness of each tool. Furthermore, the analysis demonstrates the capability of these tools to uncover hidden content across multiple formats, including text, audio, video, PDF, and images.

References

[1] Johnson, N. F., & Jajodia, S. (1998, April). Steganalysis of images created using current steganography software. In *International Workshop on Information Hiding* (pp. 273–289). Springer Berlin Heidelberg.

[2] Dalal, M., & Juneja, M. (2021). Steganography and steganalysis (in digital forensics): A cybersecurity guide. *Multimedia Tools and Applications*, *80*(4), 5723–5771.

[3] Avcibas, I., Memon, N., & Sankur, B. (2003). Steganalysis using image quality metrics. *IEEE Transactions on Image Processing*, *12*(2), 221–229.

[4] Chutani, S., & Goyal, A. (2019). A review of forensic approaches to digital image Steganalysis. *Multimedia Tools and Applications*, *78*(13), 18169–18204.

[5] Cheddad, A., Condell, J., Curran, K., & Mc Kevitt, P. (2007, October). A comparative analysis of steganographic tools. In *Proceedings of the Seventh IT&T Conference. Institute of Technology Blanchardstown, Dublin, Ireland* (pp. 29–37).

[6] Chen, M., Zhang, R., Niu, X., & Yang, Y. (2006, December). Analysis of current steganography tools: Classifications & features. In *2006 International Conference on Intelligent Information Hiding and Multimedia* (pp. 384–387). IEEE.

[7] Reinel, T. S., Raul, R. P., & Gustavo, I. (2019). Deep learning applied to steganalysis of digital images: A systematic review. *IEEE Access*, *7*, 68970–68990.

[8] Kumar, P. V. (2016, May). StegAnalyzer—An efficient spatial domain steganalysis tool. In *2016 International Conference on Advanced Communication Control and Computing Technologies)* (pp. 512–515). IEEE.

[9] Banerjee, I., Bhattacharyya, S., & Sanyal, G. (2013). Study and analysis of text steganography tools. *International Journal of Computer Network and Information Security*, *5*(12), 45.

[10] Leila, B., Mohamed, D., & Ahmed, B. (2016). A comparative study of steganography and steganalysis tools. *Algerian Journal of Signals and Systems*, *1*(2), 92–98.

[11] Veena, S. T., & Arivazhagan, S. (2021). Forensic steganalysis for identification of steganography software tools using multiple format image. *International Journal of Informatics and Communication Technology*, *2252*(8776), 189.

[12] Meghanathan, N., & Nayak, L. (2010). Steganalysis algorithms for detecting the hidden information in image, audio, and video cover media. *International Journal of Network Security & Its Application*, *2*(1), 43–55.

[13] Ye, J., Ni, J., & Yi, Y. (2017). Deep learning hierarchical representations for image steganalysis. *IEEE Transactions on Information Forensics and Security*, *12*(11), 2545–2557.

[14] Shojae Chaeikar, S., Zamani, M., Abdul Manaf, A. B., & Zeki, A. M. (2018). PSW statistical LSB image steganalysis. *Multimedia Tools and Applications*, *77*(1), 805–835.

[15] Pilania, U., Tanwar, R., & Gupta, P. (2021). Performance analysis of open-source image steganography tools. *Journal of Engineering and Applied Sciences*, *8*(1), 57–67.

[16]. Pilania, U., Tanwar, R., Gupta, P., & Choudhury, T. (2021). A roadmap of steganography tools: Conventional to modern. *Spatial Information Research*, *29*(5), 761–774.

[17]. Pilania, U., Tanwar, R., & Kaushik, K. (2022, June). Steganography tools and their analysis concerning distortion in stego image. In *International Conference on Advances in Data Science and Computing Technologies* (pp. 531–538). Springer Nature Singapore.

7

Exploring Steganography Tools for Embedding Secret Multimedia Files

7.1 Introduction

Steganography is the process of embedding the secret information inside the cover file so that no one is aware of the existence of the secret message. In ancient times, classical methods were used to hide secret messages, but in this digital era, many modern tools can embed it. The tools available can embed a secret message in any multimedia form, such as text, image, PDF, audio, video, etc. These tools are user-friendly and straightforward to operate. These tools provide multi-layer security to the secret information. The tools work similarly to the steganography techniques. These tools ensure the secret information's integrity, confidentiality, and authenticity [1, 2]. Details of some of the tools are given as follows:

7.1.1 *OpenStego*

It is the most commonly used steganography tool to hide secret data. It can conceal data and do watermarking. It takes secret information as text, image, or audio as the cover file. Output is generated in the form of a stego-image. For more security, it uses AES encryption. The tool is written in Java, so a Java installation is its primary requirement. It works efficiently on Windows and Linux environments. It supports AES of 128 and 256 bits. It embeds the secret data using randomized LSB, DCT, FFT, and Dugad algorithms. CMD can also embed secret information [3, 4].

Figure 7.1 depicts the workflow of concealing a secret message within a cover file. In this process, the hidden message is taken as a

DOI: 10.1201/9781003504139-7

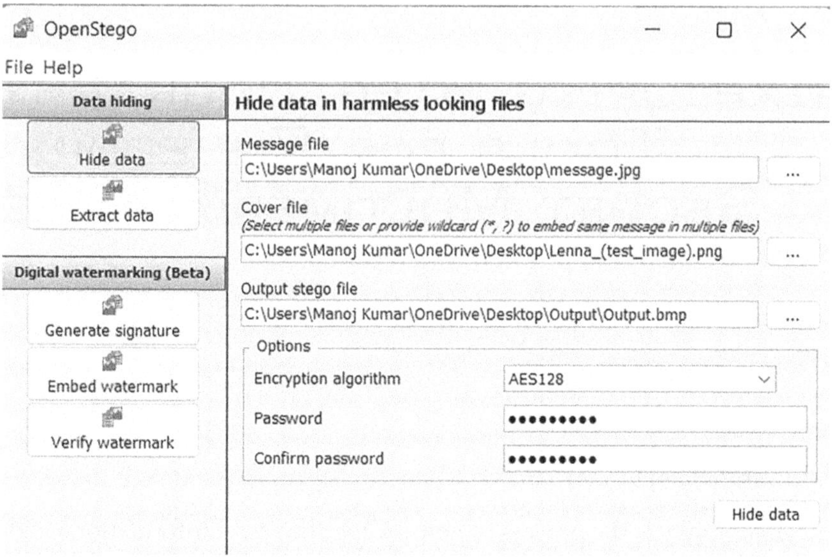

Figure 7.1 Information hiding process flow.

JPG image, while the cover file is an image in PNG format. The output generated is a stego image with a BMP extension. The LSB technique is applied to substitute the bits of the secret message in the LSB bits of the cover file. The hidden information is protected using the AES-128 encryption algorithm and a password to ensure higher security. Figure 7.2 shows the generated stego file, which is later used at the receiver's end for message extraction.

Figure 7.3 illustrates retrieving the secret message by providing the correct password. As shown in Figure 7.4, the extracted message is obtained as a JPG image. Figure 7.5 presents the retrieved image, which retains high quality, demonstrating the steganography tool's robustness and reliability. The balance between concealing capacity, robustness, and visual quality of stego is a must. When one parameter was changed among the mentioned parameters, the other two were automatically affected, resulting in a poor steganography technique.

7.1.2 OpenPuff

It is the first steganography tool, designed in 2004 for Windows, with a size varying from 256 MB to 512 MB. OpenPuff is a portable software

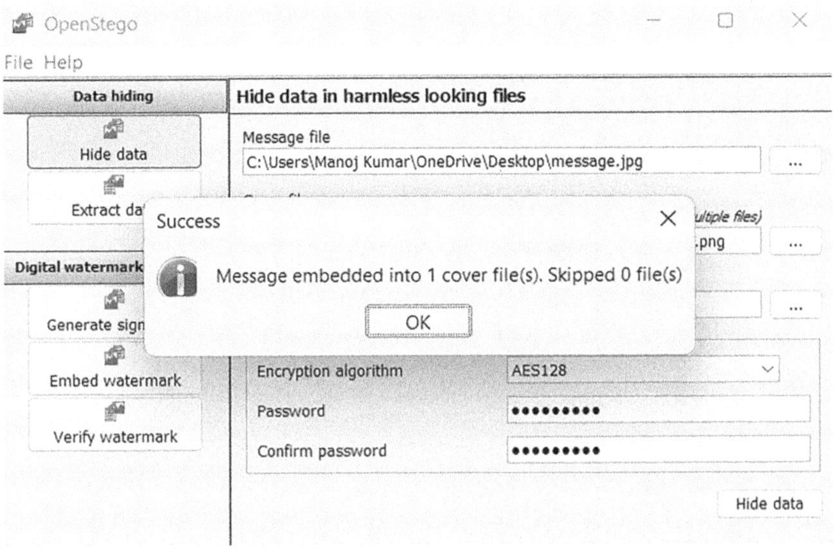

Figure 7.2 Hidden secret data.

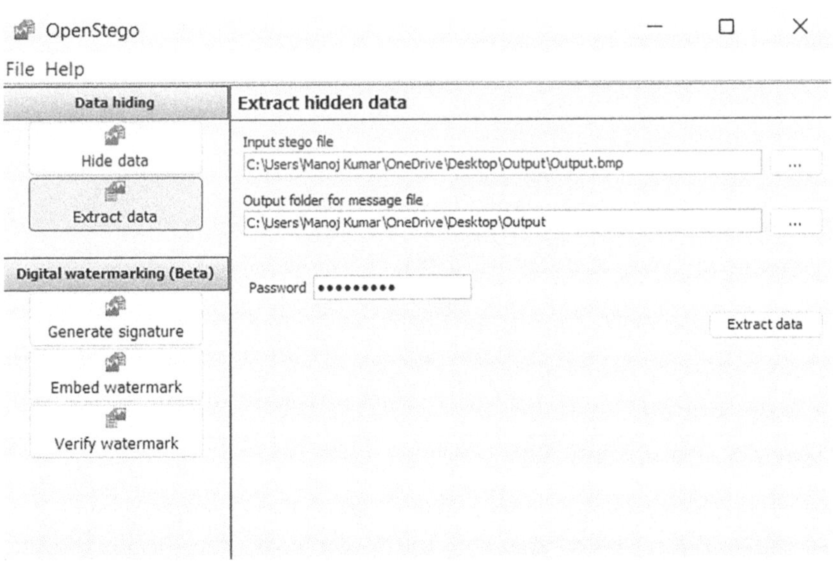

Figure 7.3 Secret message retrieval.

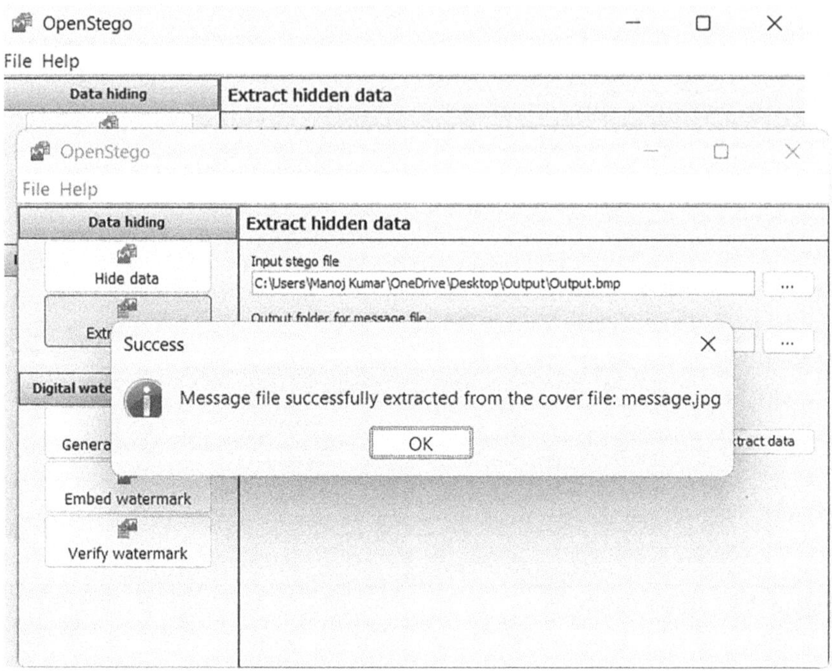

Figure 7.4 Retrieved jpg secret image.

Figure 7.5 Retrieved secret image.

for embedding a secret message inside the cover file. It can hide up to 256 MB of data in any suitable cover file. Cover files may include images, audio, video, and PDF formats. It provides four levels of security, including cryptography, scrambling, whitening, and encoding [5, 6]. Figure 7.6 illustrates the process of embedding a secret message using the OpenPuff tool, where a PNG image is used as the secret file and a JPEG image serves as the cover file. Figures 7.7 and 7.8 show

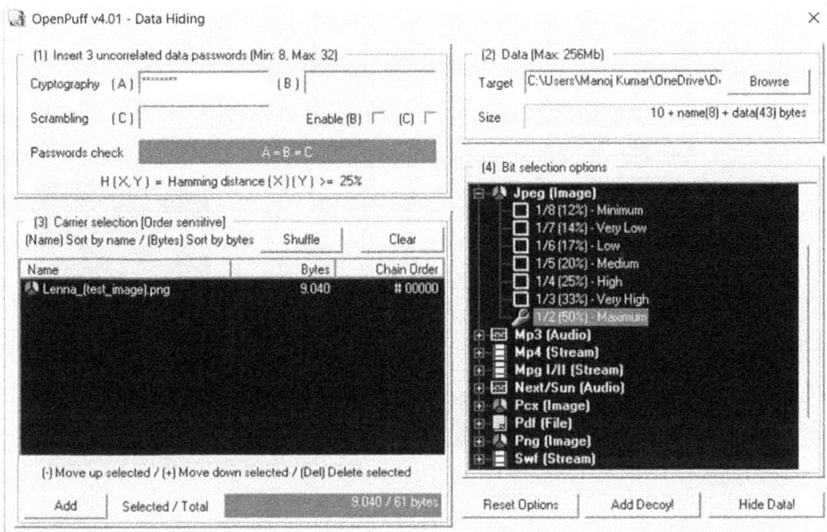

Figure 7.6 Secret information hiding.

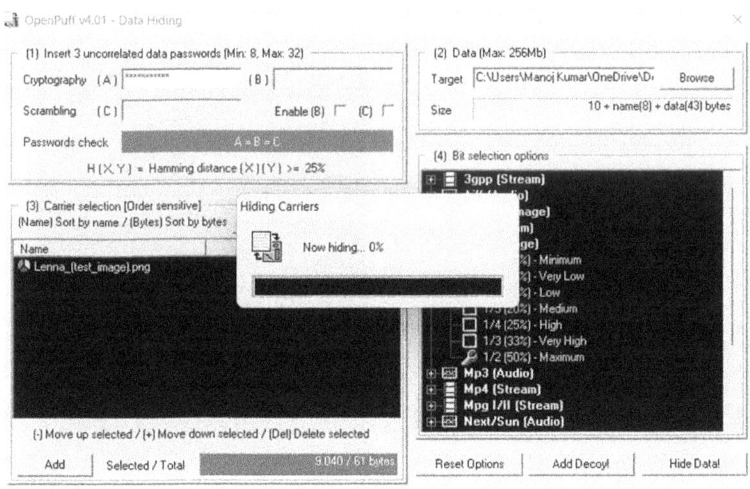

Figure 7.7 Hidden secret information.

the hidden secret message within the JPEG cover image. Figure 7.9 demonstrates the process of retrieving the concealed information, while Figures 7.10 and 7.11 depict the complete workflow at the receiver's end. The tool is found to be robust against image-processing attacks, as it is protected by different mechanisms at different levels.

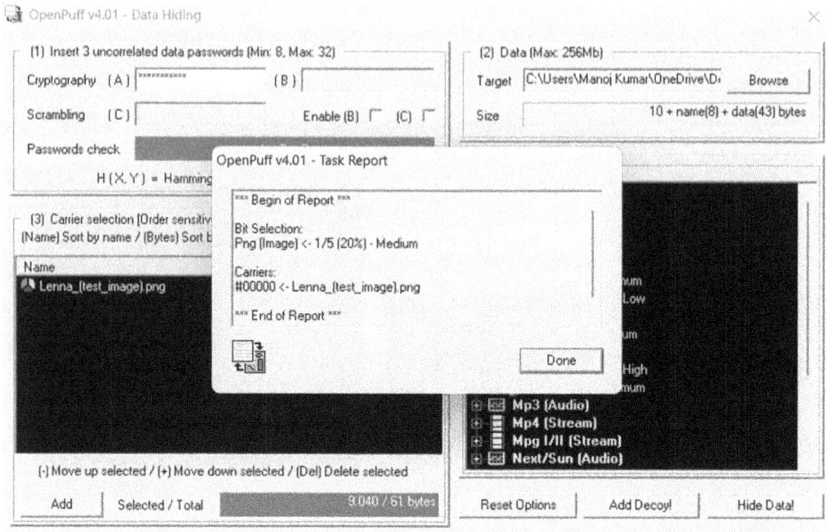

Figure 7.8 Hidden information.

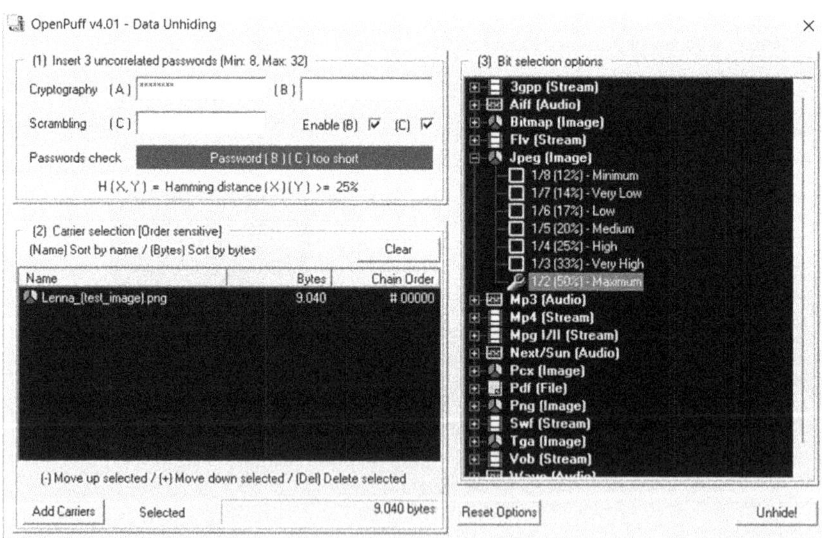

Figure 7.9 Secret information retrieval process.

7.1.3 Steghide

StegOnline is an open-source, browser-based tool designed to embed secret messages within cover image files, eliminating the need for installation. Developed by George Om, it employs the LSB method

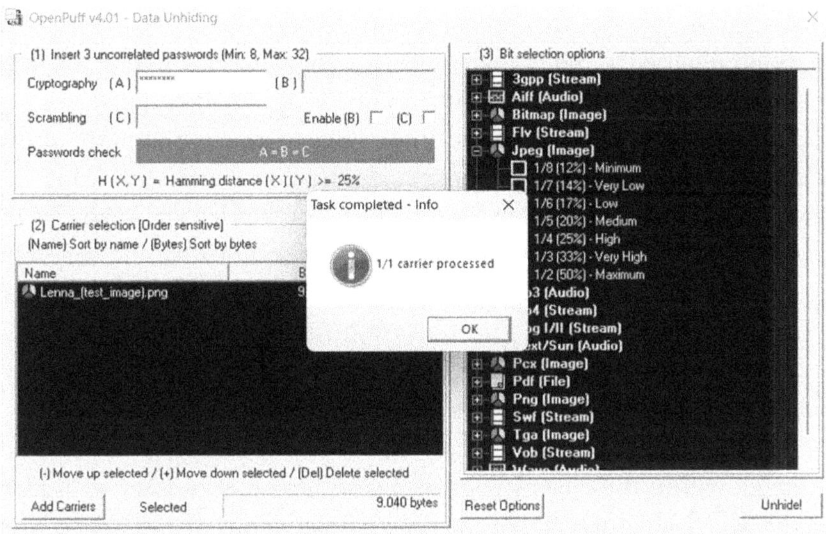

Figure 7.10 Password protect at receiver side.

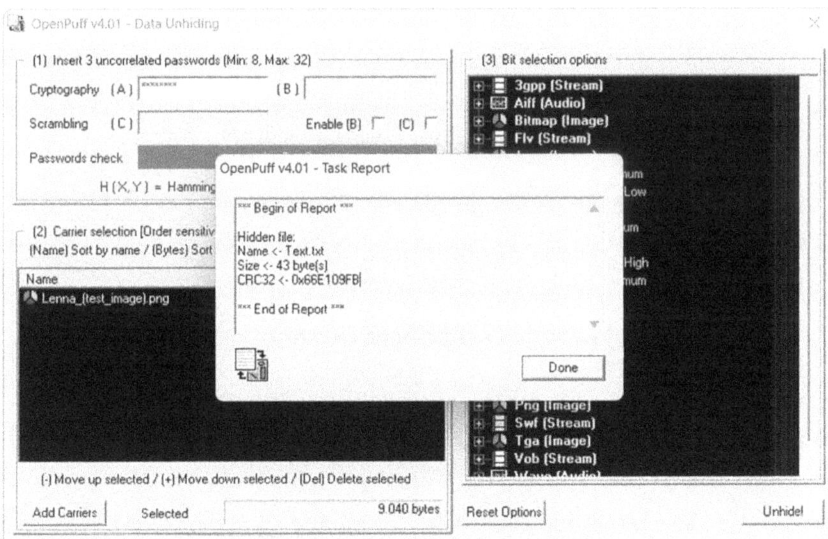

Figure 7.11 Retrieved secret information.

to hide messages within the RGB channels of an image. The cover file is an image (in PNG or BMP format), while the secret message is provided as text [7]. The LSB is the most straightforward technique, replacing the least significant bits of the cover file with the hidden message bits. It is not very robust against image-processing attacks due to its simplicity. The 3 bits of the message are concealed in red, the next 3 bits in green, and the last 2 bits in blue of the RGB channel.

During embedding, the secret message is concealed in parts of the image that do not significantly affect its visual properties, ensuring the cover image remains visually unchanged. The hidden message can be extracted at the receiver's end, maintaining good quality and integrity [8]. At the receiver end, the reverse process occurs, and the retrieved message's quality decides the tool's robustness. If the retrieved file is almost the same as the stego message, there are fewer chances of detecting the hidden secret message.

Figure 7.12 illustrates the process of embedding a secret text message within the cover image, showing how the message is hidden in the RGB channels based on the characteristics of the secret text. Figure 7.13 depicts the statistical changes in the cover image after

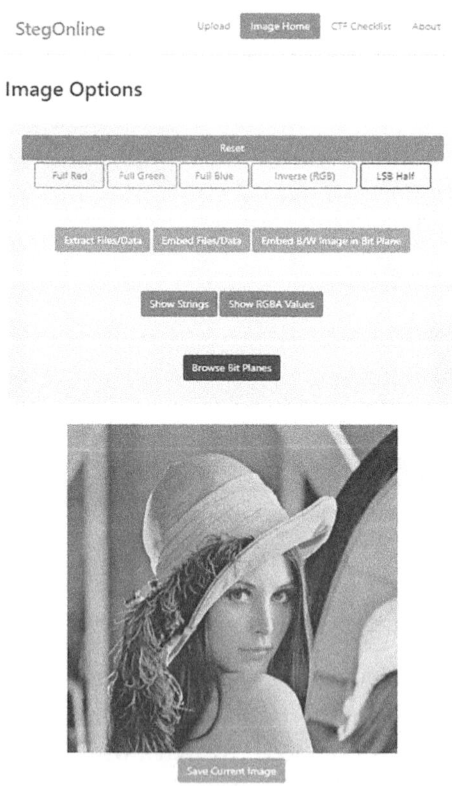

Figure 7.12 Secret message embedding.

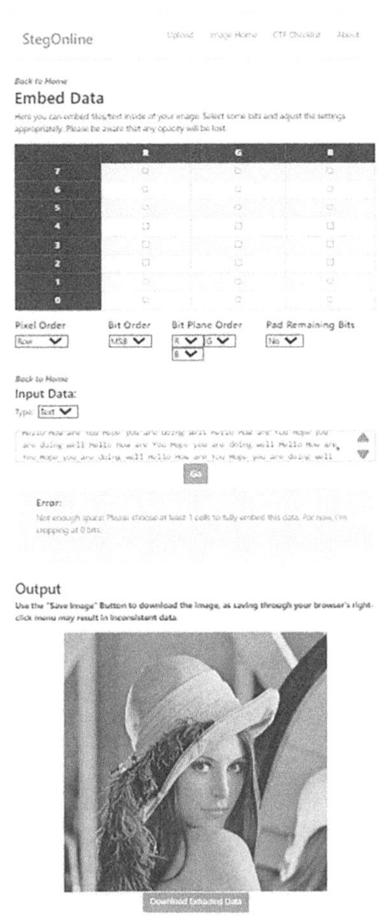

Figure 7.13 Changes in statistical properties.

embedding. To retrieve the hidden message, the receiver applies the reverse process to extract the secret text from the stego-image. The similarity between the cover and stego images shows that the third party is unaware of the hidden secret message.

The tool is robust if the statistical properties do not change much when hiding and retrieving the secret message. When a large amount of secret data is hidden, the visual quality of the stego may degrade, resulting in exposure to the steganography tool. The trade-off between the concealing capacity, visual quality of the stego, and robustness against attacks plays an essential role in steganography tools. When changing any of the parameters, the other two automatically get affected.

7.1.4 QuickStego

It is an open-source steganography tool for the Windows operating system. It has approximately a 2MB window size. It can embed text messages inside images in different formats. It does not use encryption techniques before embedding the message. Its advanced version is QuickCrypto, which uses cryptography on a secret message and then embeds it. It uses LSB steganography to embed the hidden message in the cover file. Least significant bits are modified to embed the secret message [9, 10].

Figure 7.14 illustrates embedding secret text information within the cover image. The cover image is shown in Figure 7.14, while the secret text is displayed in Figure 7.15. Figure 7.16 demonstrates the text successfully hidden inside the cover image. In Figure 7.17, the secret data is extracted from the cover image. The quality of the stego-image closely matches that of the original cover image, indicating that the tool is robust and reliable for concealing secret information.

Figure 7.14 Cover image.

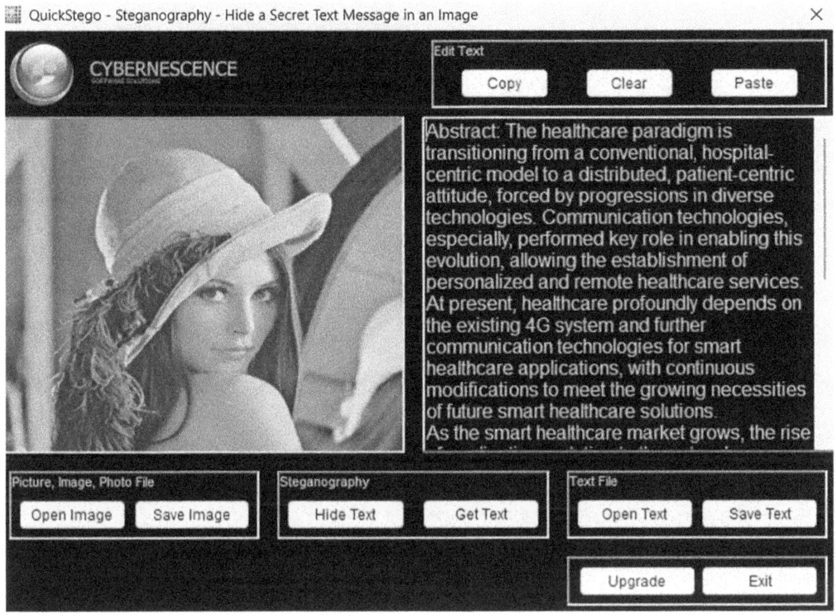

Figure 7.15 Secret text.

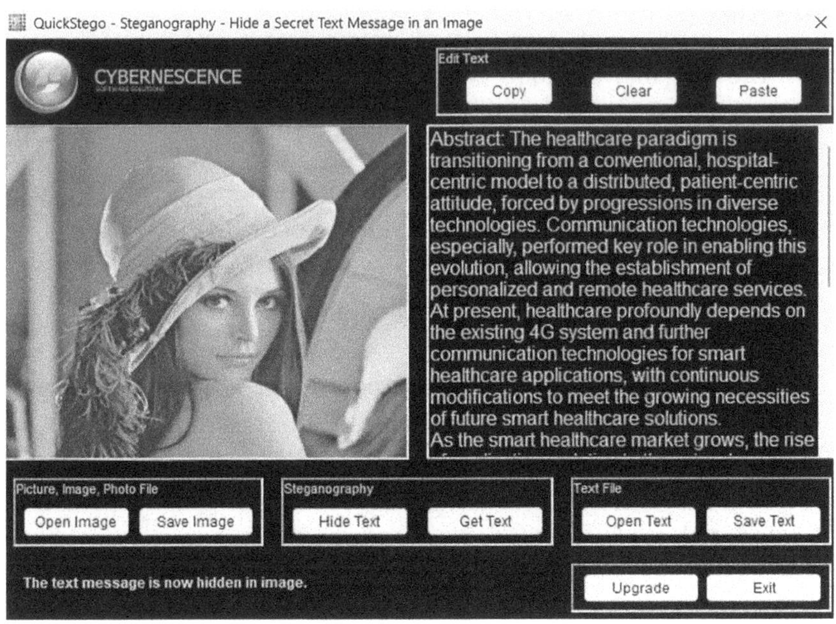

Figure 7.16 Embedding secret data.

Figure 7.17 Cover image after secret message extraction.

7.2 Challenges with Steganography Tools

Some of the challenges that still exist with steganography tools are listed below:

- The steganalysis tools are growing daily due to advances in technology. So, it isn't easy to keep the embedded data undetectable [11].
- Some of these tools can hide a minimal amount of data. When a large amount of data is embedded, the quality of the stego-image degrades, resulting in the exposure of secret data [12].
- Some tools work on a specific file type, or some cannot handle various formats [13].
- In some tools, hidden data is exposed when different attacks are applied to the stego file, such as compression [14, 15].
- In some tools, the data-hiding process is complex and requires detailed technical knowledge of the steganography process [16, 17].

7.3 Conclusion

Steganography tools add a layer of security to digital data by using techniques such as LSB, MSB, DWT, and DCT to embed secret information. These tools also use cryptography techniques and password protection to protect secret data. Within multimedia cover files, these tools can hide data in multiple formats—including text, images, PDFs, and audio. It has been observed that the quality of the cover file and the resulting stego file remains nearly identical, demonstrating the robustness of these steganography tools. Among the four tools evaluated, OpenPuff stands out as the most reliable and efficient due to its four levels of security and its ability to handle data in multiple formats and across different types of multimedia files. However, many challenges exist with the steganography tools, which cause the detection of hidden secret messages.

References

[1] Chen, M., Zhang, R., Niu, X., & Yang, Y. (2006, December). Analysis of current steganography tools: Classifications & features. In the *2006 International Conference on Intelligent Information Hiding and Multimedia* (pp. 384–387). IEEE.

[2] Sloan, T., & Hernandez-Castro, J. (2015). Forensic analysis of video steganography tools. *PeerJ Computer Science*, *1*, e7.

[3] Cheddad, A., Condell, J., Curran, K., & Mc Kevitt, P. (2007, October). A comparative analysis of steganographic tools. In *Proceedings of the Seventh IT&T Conference. Institute of Technology Blanchardstown, Dublin, Ireland. 25th* (pp. 29–37).

[4] Kundu, D., & Upreti, A. (2018, October). Study of various steganography tools. In *2018 International Conference on Automation and Computational Engineering (ICACE)* (pp. 117–120). IEEE.

[5] Banerjee, I., Bhattacharyya, S., & Sanyal, G. (2013). Study and analysis of text steganography tools. *International Journal of Computer Network and Information Security*, *5*(12), 45.

[6] Pilania, U., Tanwar, R., & Gupta, P. (2021). Performance analysis of open-source image steganography tools. *Journal of Engineering and Applied Sciences*, *8*(1), 50–67.

[7] Pilania, U., Tanwar, R., Gupta, P., & Choudhury, T. (2021). A roadmap of steganography tools: Conventional to modern. *Spatial Information Research*, *29*(5), 761–774.

[8] Pope, M. B., Warkentin, M., Bekkering, E., & Schmidt, M. B. (2012). Digital steganography—An introduction to techniques and tools. *Communications of the Association for Information Systems*, *30*(1), 22.

[9] Dalal, M., & Juneja, M. (2021). Steganography and steganalysis (in digital forensics): a Cybersecurity guide. *Multimedia Tools and Applications*, *80*(4), 5723–5771.

[10] Islam, M. A., Riad, M. A. A. K., & Pias, T. S. (2020, November). Performance analysis of steganography tools. In *2020 2nd International Conference on Advanced Information and Communication Technology* (pp. 428–433). IEEE.
[11] Das, R. (2014). An investigation on information hiding tools for steganography. *International Journal of Information Security Science, 3*(3), 200–208.
[12] Yari, I. A., & Zargari, S. (2017, June). An overview and computer forensic challenges in image steganography. In *2017 IEEE International Conference on Internet of Things (iThings) and IEEE Green Computing and Communications (GreenCom) and IEEE Cyber, Physical and Social Computing (CPSCom) and IEEE Smart Data (SmartData)* (pp. 360–364). IEEE.
[13] Bachrach, M., & Shih, F. Y. (2011). Image steganography and steganalysis. *Wiley Interdisciplinary Reviews: Computational Statistics, 3*(3), 251–259.
[14] Westfeld, A., & Pfitzmann, A. (1999, September). Attacks on steganographic systems: Breaking the steganographic utilities EzStego, Jsteg, Steganos, and S-Tools-and some lessons learned. In *International Workshop on Information Hiding* (pp. 61–76). Springer Berlin Heidelberg.
[15] Arora, N. (2022). Types and tools of steganography. *International Journal for Research in Applied Science & Engineering Technology, 10*(6), 2049–2053.
[16] Pilania, U., Tanwar, R., & Kaushik, K. (2022, June). Steganography tools and their analysis concerning distortion in stego image. In *International Conference on Advances in Data Science and Computing Technologies* (pp. 531–538). Springer Nature Singapore.
[17] Pilania, U., Kumar, M., & Mittal, V. (2023). Performance evaluation of LSB steganography based on multiple image formats. *Journal of Discrete Mathematical Sciences and Cryptography, 26*(7), 1911–1924.

8

Secret Information Hiding in Images Using LSB and X-Box Method

8.1 Introduction

The information exchange on the web has become very common these days due to the advancement in technology and awareness in the people. These days everyone is using web to share or transmit the information [1]. So security of sensitive information is necessary and it is actually a challenge for the researchers. Steganography can be used to address this challenge. It can be defined as the process of hiding secret data within the carrier file. In this chapter images are taken as cover file and text is taken as the secret data. The images which are taken as carrier is used in multiple formats to validate the research work. In this work, LSB is used to hide the secret data in carrier image. LSB replace the least significant bits by the bits of secret data. It is simple to implement but not much robust against attacks [2]. So to increase the robustness authors also used X-Box technique along with LSB.

The steganography techniques can be assessed through concealing capacity, visual quality of stego, and robustness against image-processing attacks. If the visual quality of the stego degrades, then the third party can detect and expose hidden information. There is a trade-off between these three parameters. On changing any one parameter other two automatically got affected. For example, if the concealing capacity is increased then the visual quality of the stego and robustness automatically degrade and may causes exposure of hidden data.

Successful steganography communication depends on choosing a suitable cover medium and selecting a secure steganography method

DOI: 10.1201/9781003504139-8

for delivering the stego object. At the receiver end the stego file is decoded to retrieve the hidden secret data. Decoding process is just the reverse process of the encoding process. Standard transmission methods include email, social media, or online platforms, where a stego image may appear publicly accessible but remains unnoticed in terms of its hidden content. This subtlety is the core strength of steganography, ensuring data confidentiality by disguising its very existence [3]. As images are most commonly transmitted or shared by the web users so image steganography is gaining attention day by day.

8.2 Objectives of Steganography

In steganography, secret information is concealed in a cover file to produce a stego file, which should visually appear identical to the original cover image. This similarity is crucial to prevent intruders' detection, ensuring that the concealed message remains unnoticed. The key objectives of the steganography process include [4]:

- Embedding a large amount of data with negligible distortion to the cover image.
- Ensuring that the stego image remains visually and statistically indistinguishable from the original.

Maintaining the integrity of the hidden message even if the stego file is partially modified or tampered with by an intruder. Modern steganography techniques aim to produce stego images that are statistically indistinguishable from unaltered images, making unauthorized detection extremely difficult and enhancing the security of covert communication [5, 6].

8.3 Scope of Research

The scope of research for the proposed chapter is as follows:

- To propose and develop an image steganography method utilizing the LSB insertion technique.
- To achieve improved performance, specifically a higher PSNR compared to existing steganography approaches.

8.4 Proposed Methodology

8.4.1 Generation of the X-Box

In the proposed work, the authors utilized X-Box to store values, as shown in Figure 8.1. Authors have taken the X-box as a 2×2 matrix. The 4 X-box has been taken to store 16 values from 0 to 15. For storing values in X-box, authors have applied the X-OR property. If, for example, we have to store the value 10 in X-Box, then it could be stored as follows: 10 in binary could be written as 1010= 10 X-O

R 10 is 0 0 hence it is stored at first row and second column.

The authors have chosen the secret information to be concealed as 132, which will be embedded within the RGB channels of an image. Each channel—Red, Green, and Blue—represents a pixel component. A key is employed to determine which color channel will be used to hide each bit of the secret data. This key repeatedly generates random values from the set {0, 1, 2} until all bits of the secret data are concealed. A key value of 0 indicates that the bit will be embedded in the Red channel, 1corresponds to the Green channel, and 2 to the Blue channel.

8.4.2 Division of Bits

Suppose we want to conceal the binary message $(11001010)_2$ in the cover file. A predefined key sequence determines the selection of pixels for embedding the data. For example, let the key sequence be: 2, 1, 0, 0, 1, 1, ... Next, divide the entire message into four parts, each consisting of 2 bits, as shown below in Figure 8.2: $(11001010)_2 = (202)_{10}$

	0	1
0	6	1
1	12	4

	0	1
0	2	8
1	14	5

	0	1
0	3	15
1	7	0

	0	1
0	9	11
1	13	10

Figure 8.1 S-box.

$$\underbrace{11}_{b_1}\quad \underbrace{00}_{b_2}\quad \underbrace{10}_{b_3}\quad \underbrace{10}_{b_4}$$

Figure 8.2 Division of bits.

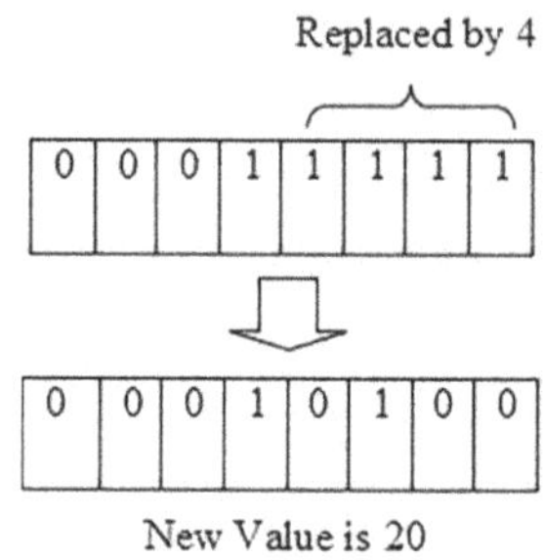

Figure 8.3 Insertion of secret message.

8.4.3 Mapping Values with X-Boxes

The X-boxes' values are matched with b_1, b_2, b_3, and b_4. Four is found when we search for the 2nd row and the 2nd column of the first X-Box value. The value four can be written in binary as $(0100)_2$. The remaining mapping values for b2 are 2, b_3 is 7, and for b_4 are 13.

8.4.4 Insertion of Bits in the Cover Image

After getting the mapping values, these values must be concealed in the LSB of the carrier file. These calculated values are inserted into the four bits of LSB sequentially. The four LSBs were substituted sequentially with 4, 2, 7, and 13 values, as shown in Figure 8.3.

Authors have taken random values for the key = 2, 1, 0, 1…. So, b_1 bits are concealed in the blue color pixel as discussed above. For example, if the blue color pixels are $(00011111)_2 = (31)_{10.}$ When we insert b_2, the key is one means of data that needs to be concealed in green color. In this way, all the secret message bits are concealed in the RGB channel.

8.4.5 Stego Image Formation

By combining the pixel values of the RGB channels, the stego file is created. The stego image carries secret information inside it. The reverse process takes place on the receiver side, and secret information is extracted from the stego image. The algorithm for concealing and extracting the secret message is given below:

Hiding algorithm

Input: Cover image will be a 24-bit RGB image of size m×n

Output: It will be a stego image of size m×n

Steps: For concealing a secret message, the following steps need to be followed:

1. Input is taken in the form of an RGB image, then divided into red, Green, and Blue pixels.
2. The message is divided into four parts, comprising two bits each.
3. The four parts obtained in step 2 are mapped with 4 X-boxes, and we got new values for every pair.
4. The new values obtained from step 3 are inserted into the LSB positions of selected color pixel values in the cover image with the help of the key.
5. A stego image is obtained by the insertion of these bits.
6. End.

8.4.6 Image Extraction

One by one, pixels of the stego image are taken, and the key is used to select the individual pixels. These pixels are converted into binary to retrieve the four LSBs. For example, in the case of $(31)_{10}$ discussed in the previous section, the pixel values generated are 0100, and so on. Can this be done for the remaining cases? These LSBs extracted will be XORed with the last two bits. When 01 X-OR 00, it will generate 01 for the remaining cases. The result is then concatenated to create the secret message.

Extraction algorithm

Input: Input the stego image of size m×n

Output: It will be a secret message

Steps: The following steps must be covered to retrieve the secret message.

1. The sender selects the key randomly.

2. Pixel values are selected according to the key from the input image, and four LSB bits are retrieved from the LSB position of every pixel.
3. Selected LSB bits go for the X-OR operation.
4. The result is concatenated.
5. End

For the execution of the proposed work, we need Microsoft Visual Studio and the .NET Framework. Visual Studio's powerful code editor supports code refactoring and offers language-specific services for multiple programming languages, enhancing productivity and development efficiency. It is also an IDE utilized for research purposes. It supports various platforms, including Windows [7, 8]. The .NET Framework is tightly integrated with Visual Studio, which enhances development productivity by offering features like background compilation, real-time syntax checking, and error highlighting [9, 10, 11]. It allows programmers to use multiple languages for programming purposes. C+ + is used as the language for the implementation of the work.

8.5 Welcome Page to Hide Information

This is the welcome page for hiding secret messages. It includes a "Hide Message" section, where users can select the carrier file. The file into which the secret message will be embedded is specified by specifying its original name and the new name under which the modified file will be saved. The "Add" button allows users to browse and select the carrier file from their computer, while the Remove button clears the previously selected file.

Additionally, there is an option to select the message file containing the secret information to be hidden. Once all inputs are provided, clicking the "Hide Message" button initiates the embedding process, generating a new stego file saved at a specified location on the user's system, as represented by Figure 8.4.

8.5.1 Page to Hide Information

After clicking the "Add" button, a new window appears displaying the selected file's name. It also includes a "save as" option, allowing the user

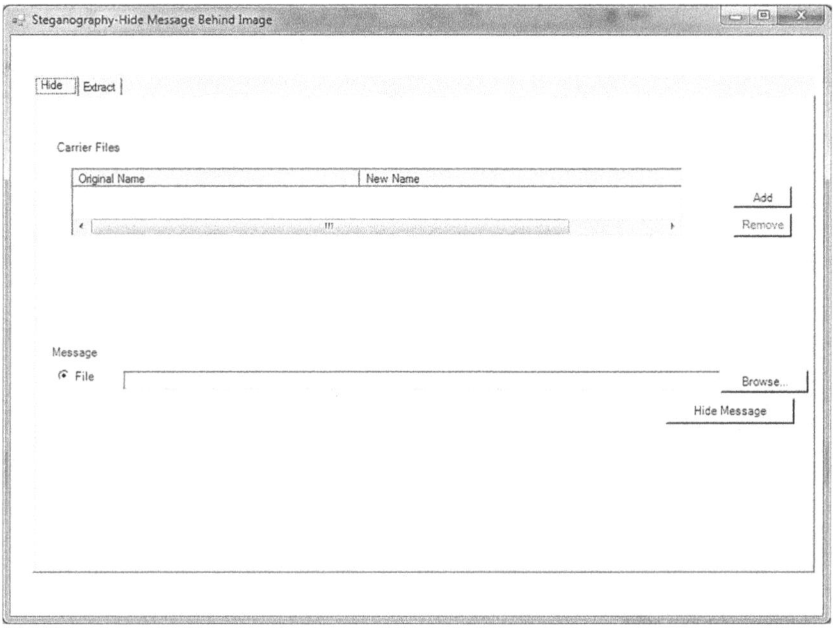

Figure 8.4 Message embedding.

to specify a new name and location for the output file. Once the save button is clicked, the user is redirected to the main "Hide Message" page, as represented by Figure 8.5. When user click on hide button then secret message got concealed in the uploaded .bmp carrier file. The cover image file can be taken in any format such as bmp, tiff, png, jpg, etc. The stego file is created and saved as m1.bmp on the desktop.

8.5.2 Page to Attach Hidden Information

After clicking the "Save" button in the previous window, the application automatically returns to the main interface, and the selected path is populated in the carrier file field. Next, the user needs to browse and select the secret message file. Once the message is selected, clicking the "Hide Message" button initiates the embedding process as shown in Figures 8.5 and 8.6. After the secret message is hidden in carrier file the new file is known as the stego file.

Stego file can be defined as the file which carry secret message in it. The quality of the stego plays an important role in accessing the

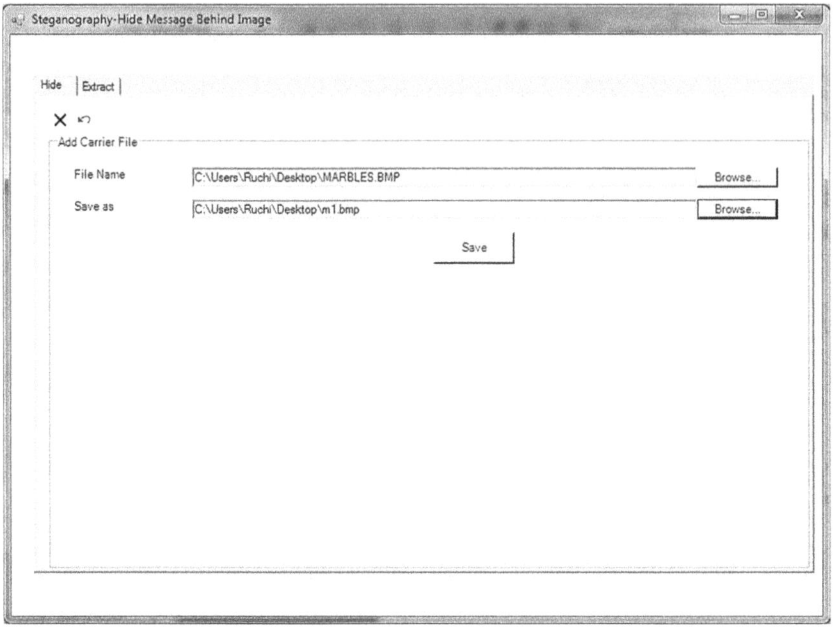

Figure 8.5 Message hidden.

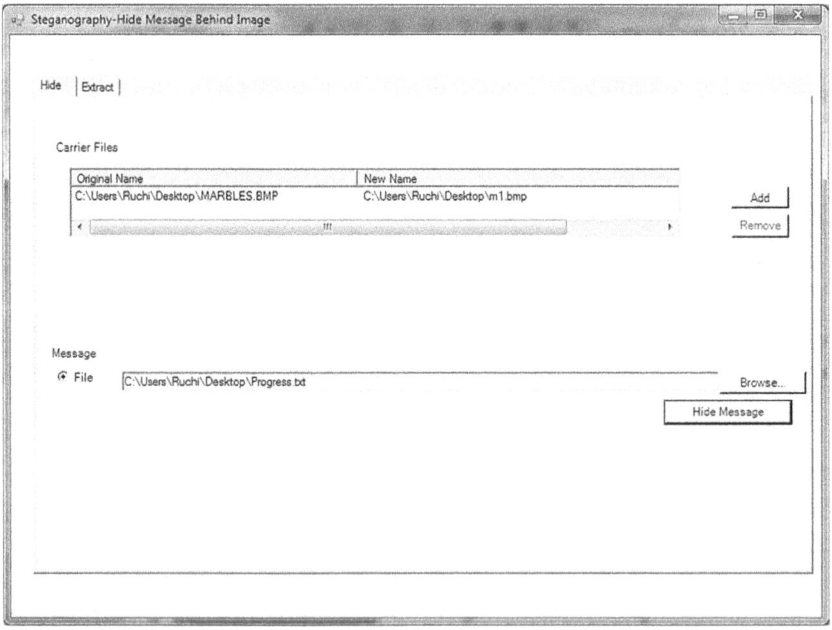

Figure 8.6 Secret message saved.

Figure 8.7 Embedded secret message.

steganography technique. If the quality of the stego file is almost similar to the carrier file then there are very less chance of detection of hidden secret data. If quality of the setgo degrades then secret message can be extracted by applying attacks on it.

The following window appears when the user clicks on the "Hide Message" button, as represented by Figure 8.7. The secret message is concealed in the carrier image. Now no one other than the sender and receiver is aware of the existence of the hidden secret data.

8.5.3 Welcome Page for the Extraction of Message

This is the welcome page for extracting a hidden message. It provides options to select the carrier file containing the embedded secret message. The "Add" button allows users to browse and select the carrier file from their computer, while the "Remove" button clears any previously selected file. The "Message" button saves the extracted secret message by assigning it a new name, preserving its original file format as shown in Figure 8.8. The extraction of secret message is just the reverse process of the embedding.

8.5.4 Page to Extract the Information

Here, the carrier file is selected, and the secret message is browsed and saved with a new name and original file format. Now, the "Extract Message" button is clicked. The following window appears after clicking the button, as shown in Figure 8.9. The quality of the extracted message plays an important role in the assessment of any steganography technique.

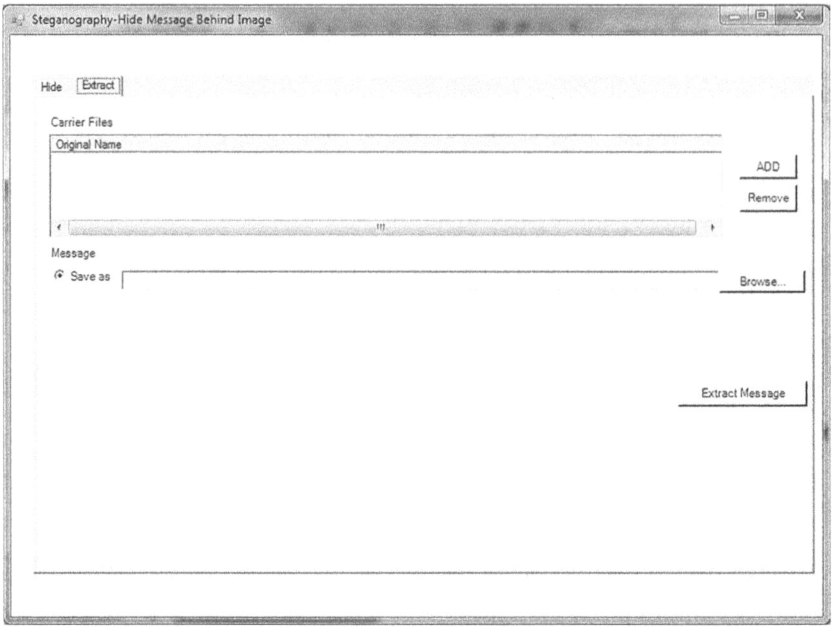

Figure 8.8 Secret message extractions.

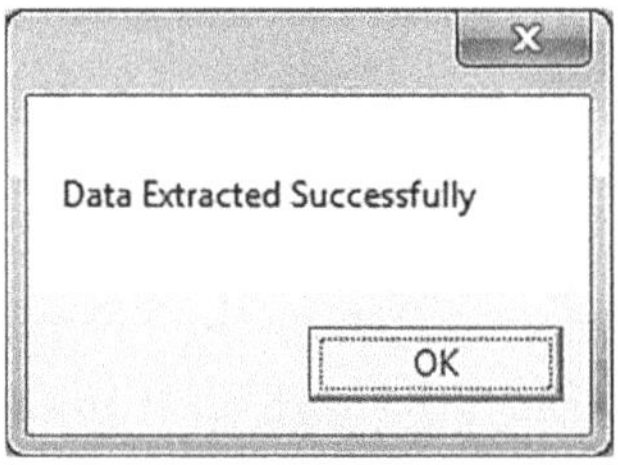

Figure 8.9 Secret message extracted successfully.

8.5.5 Snapshots for PSNR Value

PSNR is used to evaluate the steganography technique. The higher the value of PSNR, the lower the chances of detecting a hidden secret message [12, 13]. The following are the snapshots for calculating the PSNR value using Equation 8.1 for Lena's image as shown in Figure 8.10. The R is the maximum possible value of the image, and MSE is the mean square error [13, 14, 15]. The PSNR value above 30dB generates good quality stego, and the hidden message is not detectable. In the proposed work, the PSNR value achieved is more than 52 dB, which means the proposed steganography technique is robust against attacks.

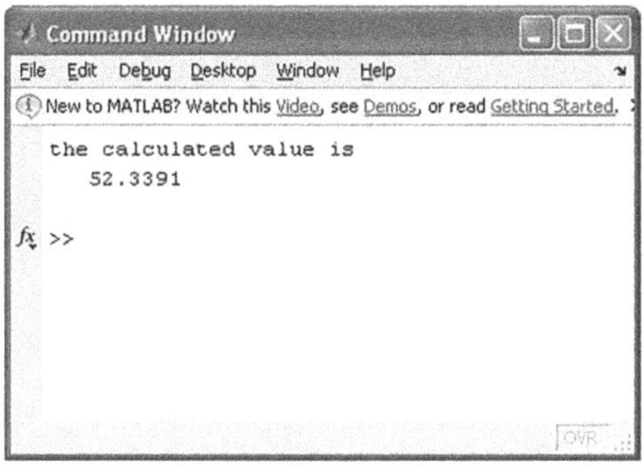

Figure 8.10 PSNR value.

$$PSNR = 10log_{10}\left(\frac{R^2}{MSE}\right) \tag{8.1}$$

8.6 Conclusion

Steganography is valuable for ensuring information security, and enabling secure and covert network communication. The experimental results demonstrate that the proposed method effectively hides secret data, offering improved performance due to integrating X-boxes. The value mapping through X-boxes enhances security by making it more difficult for unauthorized users to detect alterations in the stego image.

The approach yields a higher PSNR value, indicating better image quality with minimal distortion. Additionally, it shows strong resistance to statistical attacks. The combined use of a key and X-boxes significantly increases the security of the hidden data, making it highly challenging for an attacker to extract the concealed information without access to both the key and the X-box values.

References

[1] Jebur, S. A., Nawar, A. K., Kadhim, L. E., & Jahefer, M. M. (2023). Hiding information in digital images using the LSB steganography technique. *International Journal of Interactive Mobile Technologies, 17*(7), 167–178.

[2] Dumre, R., & Dave, A. (2021, July). Exploring LSB steganography possibilities in RGB images. In *2021, the 12th International Conference on Computing, Communication, and Networking Technologies* (pp. 1–7). IEEE.

[3] Kumar, M., Soni, A., Shekhawat, A. R. S., & Rawat, A. (2022, February). Enhanced digital image text data security using a hybrid model of LSB steganography and AES cryptography technique. In *2022 Second international Conference on Artificial Intelligence and Smart Energy* (pp. 1453–1457). IEEE.

[4] Pilania, U., Tanwar, R., & Gupta, P. (2022). An ROI-based robust video steganography technique using SVD in wavelet domain. *Open Computer Science*, *12*(1), 1–16.

[5] Pilania, U., Kumar, M., Singh, S., Futela, S., & Jha, N. (2023, December). A text encryption approach for IoT devices to prioritize security and efficiency. In *International Conference on Advancements in Smart Computing and Information Security* (pp. 62–70). Springer Nature Switzerland.

[6] Hashem, M. H. A., Aljack, S. E. D., & Bahaidara, O. A. (2022). A review on RGB image steganography based on spatial domain. *University of Aden Journal of Natural and Applied Sciences*, *26*(2), 227–238.

[7] Mahmood, M. A., & Tabassum, T. (2021, December). A hybrid cryptographic data security system utilizing fuzzy vault key. In *2021 IEEE International Conference on Robotics, Automation, Artificial-Intelligence and Internet-of-Things (RAAICON)* (pp. 89–93). IEEE.

[8] Rathore, M. S., Poongodi, M., Saurabh, P., Lilhore, U. K., Bourouis, S., Alhakami, W., ... & Hamdi, M. (2022). A novel trust-based security and privacy model for internet of vehicles using encryption and steganography. *Computers and Electrical Engineering*, *102*, 108205.

[9] Hamza, A., Shehzad, D., Sarfraz, M. S., Habib, U., & Shafi, N. (2021). Novel secure hybrid image steganography technique based on pattern matching. *KSII Transactions on Internet and Information Systems*, *15*(3), 1051–1077.

[10] Abikoye, O. C., & Ogundokun, R. O. (2021). Efficiency of LSB steganography on medical information. *International Journal of Electrical and Computer Engineering)*, *11*(5), 4157–4164.

[11] Gupta, L. K., Singh, A., Kushwaha, A., & Vishwakarma, A. (2021, February). Analysis of image steganography techniques for different image format. In *2021 International Conference on Advances in Electrical, Computing, Communication and Sustainable Technologies (ICAECT)* (pp. 1–6). IEEE.

[12] Voleti, L., Balajee, R. M., Vallepu, S. K., Bayoju, K., & Srinivas, D. (2021, March). A secure image steganography using improved LSB technique and Vigenere cipher algorithm. In *2021 International Conference on Artificial Intelligence and Smart Systems)* (pp. 1005–1010). IEEE.

[13] Pilania, U., Kumar, M., & Mittal, V. (2023). Performance evaluation of LSB steganography based on multiple image formats. *Journal of Discrete Mathematical Sciences and Cryptography*, *26*(7), 1911–1924.

[14] Pilania, U., Kumar, M., Singh, S., & Mittal, V. (2023, June). Video steganography in IoT: Information embedding using OpenCV and 2LSB. In *2023 International Conference on Sustainable Computing and Smart Systems (ICSCSS)* (pp. 1067–1072). IEEE.
[15] Karim, S. M., Rahman, M. S., & Hossain, M. I. (2011, December). A new approach for LSB-based image steganography using secret key. In *14th international conference on computer and information technology (ICCIT 2011)* (pp. 286–291). IEEE.

9

Image Steganography Using LSB and Encryption Keys for Safety of Sensitive Information

9.1 Introduction

Information security has been a critical component of communication and information technology since the advent of the Internet. To protect the confidentiality of communication, cryptography was developed. Various techniques already exist for the encryption and decryption of data to maintain the confidentiality of the message. Regretfully, there are situations when keeping a message's existence secret is just as important as keeping its contents secret. Steganography is the method used to carry this out [1].

The science and art of invisible communication is known as steganography. This can be attained by hiding data in a cover file, thereby hiding the presence of the conveyed information. The Greek terms "stegos," which means "cover," and "graphy," which means "writing," are the origin of the word "steganography," which means "covered writing" [2]. In steganography, secret information can be taken as text, PDF, image, audio, or video. Similarly, a cover can have different forms such as text, photo, audio, video, and many more.

There is a long history of the concept and practice of concealing information. Herodotus, a Greek historian, describes a nobleman named Histiaeus in *Histories* who had to speak with his son-in-law in Greece. One of his most reliable slaves shaved his head, and the

DOI: 10.1201/9781003504139-9

message was permanently inked on the enslaved person's scalp. Once the enslaved person's hair regrew, he was sent out with the secret message [3]. The Germans developed the Microdot method during World War II. Information was shrunk to the size of a typed period, with photographs in particular. Sent over an unprotected channel, a typical cover message with one of the periods on the paper carrying secret data was tricky to spot [4]. Steganography is primarily utilized on computers nowadays, where networks serve as high-speed delivery channels and digital data as carriers.

Steganography and cryptography are different, as steganography focuses on preserving the existence of a message, whereas cryptography focuses on protecting the contents of a message [5]. Although cryptography and steganography can shield data from unauthorized access, neither technology is infallible and is susceptible to hacking. Part of steganography's goal is lost once concealed data are exposed [6]. So, integrating steganography with cryptography can enhance the safety of sensitive data.

Watermarking and fingerprinting methods could also be utilized instead of steganography [7]. The algorithms for these methods differ from those for steganography because they primarily focus on protecting intellectual property. Below, we will talk about these qualities of a good steganography algorithm. Every instance of an object is "marked" similarly when watermarking. When using watermarking, the sort of data packed in things is often a mark to show where it comes from or who owns it for copyright safety [8]. With fingerprinting, on the other hand , different special signs are stuck in separate copies of the object that go to various buyers. This helps the owner of ideas know who goes against their license deal by giving the property to others [8]

In watermarking and fingerprinting, the idea that data are concealed in the files might be known to everyone at times; it could even be clear, but in steganography, not being noticed is very important. A good attack on a steganography system means an enemy sees data embedded in a cover file. In contrast, a good attack on a watermarking or fingerprinting technique will not find the mark, but take it away [9].

The proposed work is evaluated based on several key parameters: robustness, PSNR value, amount of secret information concealed, reliability, and the visual quality of the stego file.

Robustness is the difficulty in detecting the hidden message and is assessed by testing the method against various image-processing attacks. Concealing capacity is determined by how much secret data can be embedded in the cover image without noticeably degrading its visual quality. PSNR is used to measure the distortion between the original and stego images. Reliability is evaluated by the method's ability to perform consistently and accurately across different platforms.

9.2 Proposed Work

In the proposed work, the authors have utilized two secret keys. These keys help conceal the secret information in the cover file so that no one is aware of the hidden secret information. The process of encrypting and decrypting secret information is shown as follows:

Encryption:

Cover File + Secret Data + Key1 + Key2 = Stego File

Decryption:

Stego File + Key1 +Key2 = Retrieved Secret Data

Key1 is the combination of 0's and 1's, which are stored in a circular 1D array as shown in Figure 9.1. The authors focused on one crucial thing: the number of 0's and 1's should be equal in the array. It will also help in providing more robustness to the proposed technique. If the number of bits in the secret information is larger than the array, it is shifted circularly to hide all the secret bits. The authors have defined key2 as having a length of eight, which can carry values varying from zero to seven. Sharing keys repeatedly with the receiver is unsafe, and it also takes resources for computation. That is why authors will use a way function to calculate Key1 for the first time, which is shared with

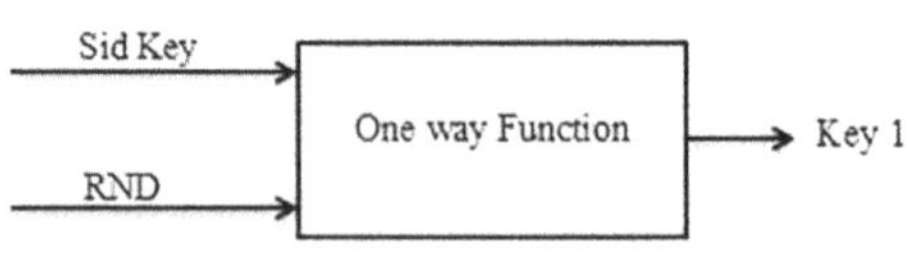

Figure 9.1 One-way function for Key1.

the receiver. The authors utilized a SID key and a random number to generate Key1. Some secret data are retrieved with key1 and the remaining with key2.

9.2.1 Concealing of Secret Data

During the concealment of secret information, both keys are utilized repeatedly as required. Initially, both keys are selected, and Key1 is XORed with the LSB of the red channel. The resulting XOR value aids in determining the placement of secret data within the green and blue channel bits. Key2 is then used to decide the specific positions for embedding the hidden information in these channels. This process is iteratively performed until the secret message is successfully embedded within the green and blue bits.

As shown in Figure 9.2, a combination of red bits and Key1 is utilized to obtain the result. Where secret information is to be embedded is decided by Key2. The same is demonstrated with the help of an example:

Suppose we have two keys as follows:

Key1 = 1, 0, 0, 1, 1, 0, 0, 1, 0 ….
Key2 = 2, 5, 1, 6, 0, 2, 1, 1, 0 ……

Let us conceal B in a cover file. ASCII value of A will be 01000001.

A = 0 1 0 0 0 0 0 1
Key2 = 2 5 1 6 0 2 1 1

From the above example it is clear that first bit of A that is '0' need to be placed at 1st bit position, second bit of A that is '0' need to be placed at 4th bit position, third bit that is '0' at 1st position, fourth bit that is '0' at 5th position, fifth bit that is '0' at 0th position, sixth bit that is '0' at 2nd position, seventh bit that '0' at 1st position and eight bit of A that is '1' will be placed at 1st position. The XOR of the LSB of the red channel and the Key1 combination will decide where these bits take place in the green and blue channels.

As illustrated in Figure 9.3, the LSB of the red channel in pixel 1 is '1', which is XORed with the first bit of Key1 located in pixel 2. The result of this XOR operation determines that the first bit of

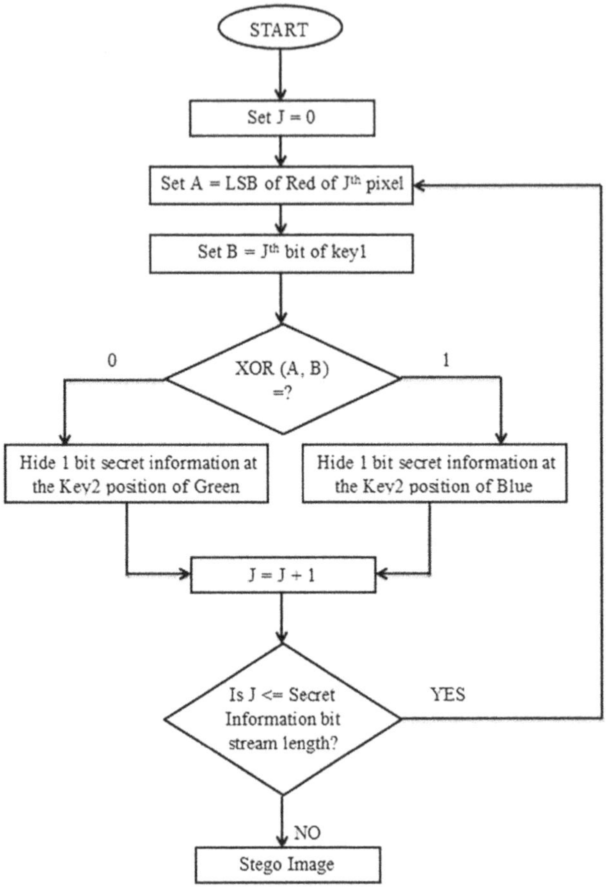

Figure 9.2 Flow chart of the hiding process.

the secret data should be embedded in the second bit of the green channel. Similarly, for pixel 2, the LSB of the red channel is XORed with the second bit of Key1. The outcome of this operation indicates the position where the next secret bit should be concealed. This process is repeated for all remaining secret message bits until the data is embedded.

9.2.2 Extraction Process

At the receiver end, the process of secret data retrieval is repeated multiple times until all the hidden information is successfully extracted.

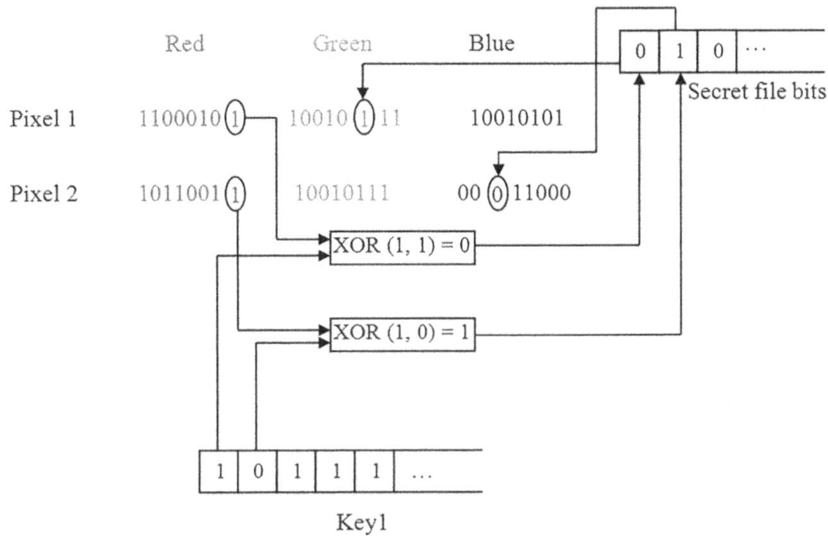

Figure 9.3 Example of hiding process.

Both secret keys determine the exact positions of the concealed data within the stego file. These keys must be securely shared with the receiver before the commencement of the extraction process. During retrieval, the LSB of the red channel is XORed with the value of Key1 to identify the position from which the corresponding secret bit is to be extracted. The secret message bits are retrieved from the green and blue channel bits. The concealing and extraction processes are designed to be equally intricate, ensuring a balanced level of complexity and security. The detailed flow of the secret data retrieval process is illustrated in Figure 9.4. Figure 9.5 explains how the hiding of a secret message takes place.

The performance of the proposed technique is determined by the visual quality of the stego file and the accuracy of the extracted secret information. To evaluate this performance, PSNR is computed, as it is one of the most widely adopted metrics by researchers for assessing the quality of stego files. A higher PSNR value indicates better image quality and reduces the likelihood of detecting the embedded secret message [10]. However, by hiding a larger quantity of secret messages, the quality of the stego file may degrade, and then the secret message can be detected by hackers.

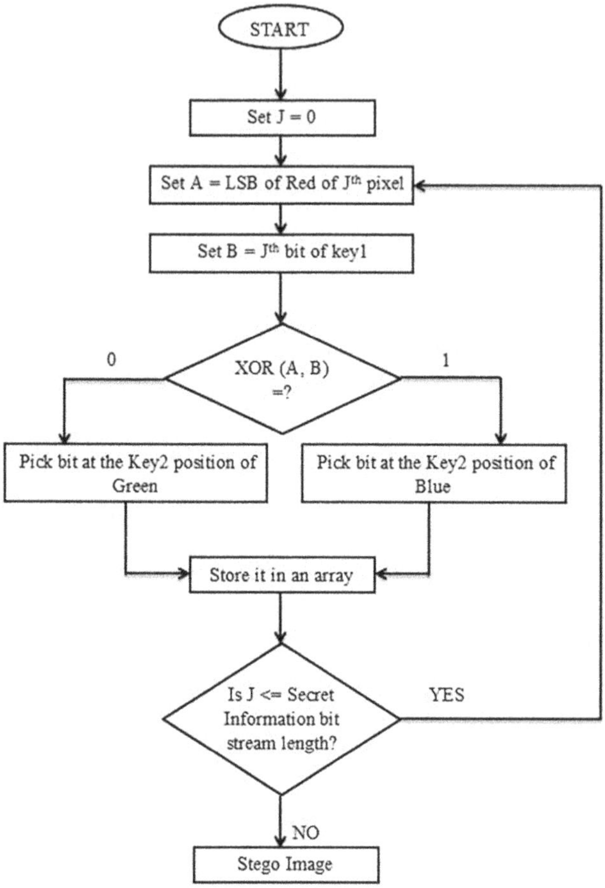

Figure 9.4 Flow chart of extraction process.

9.3 Result and Discussion

Microsoft Visual Studio (MVS) and MATLAB have been utilized at the front-end in research work. MVS helps deliver an instinctive interface for developing user interactions and executing control logic [11]. MATLAB helps in providing image processing tasks. It is known as a powerful tool for computation and visual representation. At the back end, Microsoft SQL Server 2005 is utilized to manage and store secret data [12]. It confirms well-organized extraction and incorporation with the front-end requests. The integration of the mentioned tools ensures a robust platform for developing and testing steganography methods [13]. These tools improve the reliability of data and provide

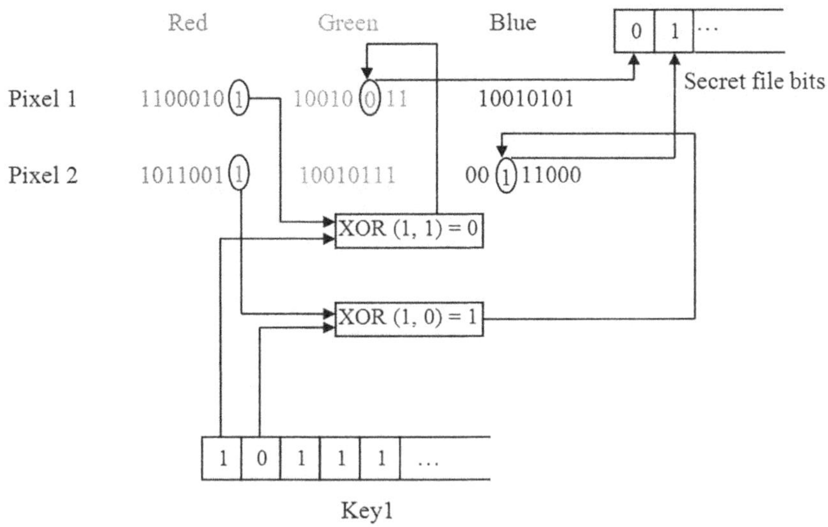

Figure 9.5 Example of hiding process.

a user-friendly environment. We have taken three images in the proposed work to conceal a secret image. The three cover images are Lena, Baboon, and Peppers. We have taken a secret image named "Baboon".

Experiment 1:

Cover Image: *lena.jpg* **Secret Image:** *baboon.jpg* **Output Image:** *lena_stego.bmp*

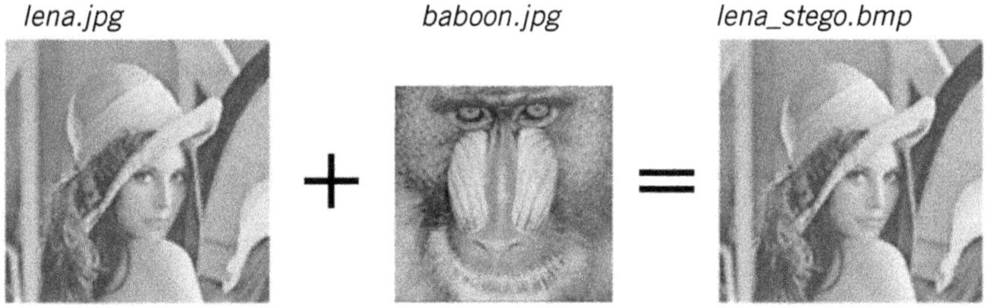

Step 1: In this step, the user has to provide a password for retrieving the secret keys, as shown in Figure 9.6. Lena's image is taken as the cover, and the monkey image is taken as the hidden file. After concealing, the stego image is generated as the Lena image. If the quality of the cover and stego is almost similar, then there are very few chances of detecting the hidden secret image.

Figure 9.6 Secret keys retrieval.

Step 2: In this step, the cover and secret files are loaded as shown in Figure 9.7 in the form available on the screen. After uploading the cover and secret image, these images are protected by the password. The user submits a password of 10 digits, letters, or special symbols.

Step 3: This step provides the path to save the stego file as shown in Figure 9.8. For the process, encryption keys are provided. All the details related to the cover file are visible on the screen, and how much data can be hidden is also shown.

Step 4: The stego file is saved successfully as shown in Figure 9.9. The URL of the stego file is required at the receiver end to extract the secret image from the stego image. The stego file is saved as a .bmp image.

Step 5: In step 5, PSNR calculations are shown in Figure 9.10. The PSNR achieved is more than 50 dB, representing the stego's high visual quality. The visual quality of stego decides whether the secret message can be detected by a third person or not [14]. The key is required to decrypt the retrieved secret message at the receiver's end. Encryption and decryption keys increase complexity but, in turn, enhance the security of the LSB steganography technique [15].

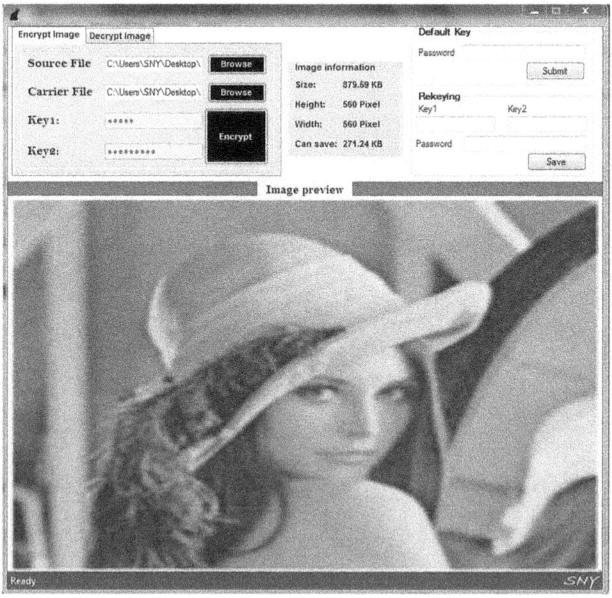

Figure 9.7 Loading of cover and secret file.

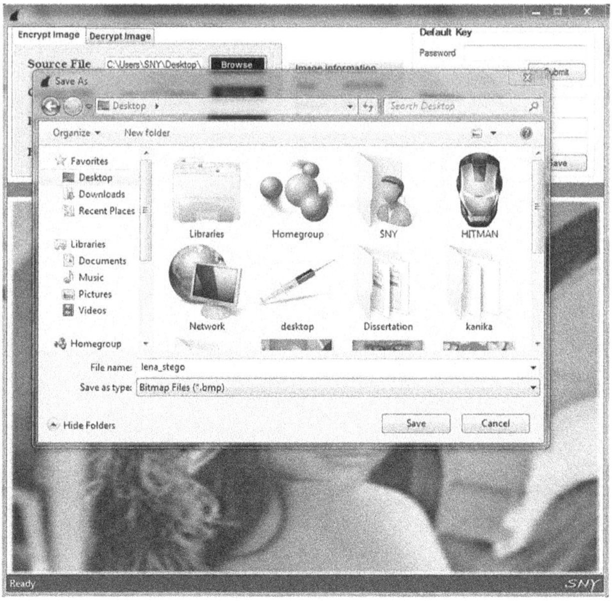

Figure 9.8 URL provided.

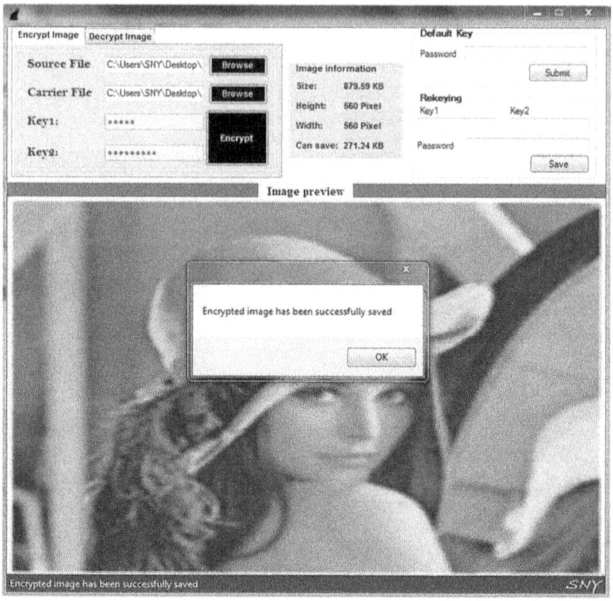

Figure 9.9 Stego file.

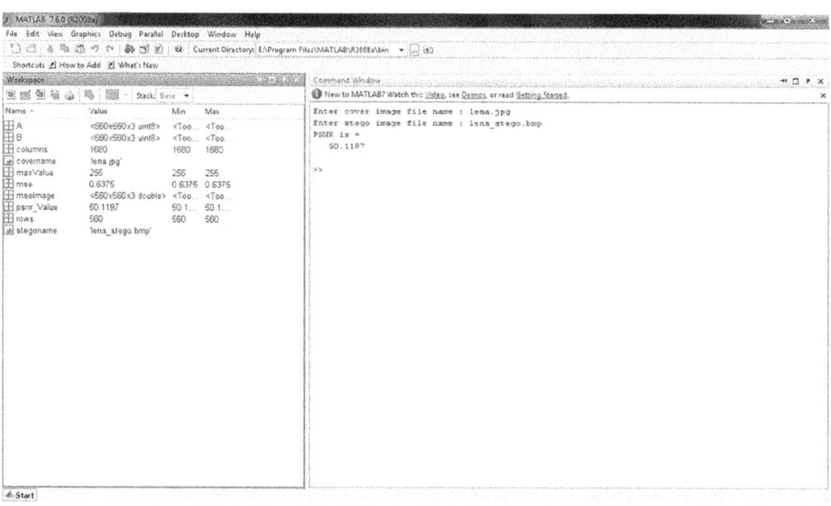

Figure 9.10 PSNR calculation.

For the proposed work, the PSNR value is calculated, and it is found to be 50.12 dB. Likewise, we have performed two more experiments. In each experiment, PSNR is calculated. For the Baboon image, the authors have calculated a PSNR value of 49.97 dB; for the Peppers image, it is estimated to be 49.99 dB. A PSNR value greater than 30 dB is considered satisfactory for the proposed steganography techniques. The higher the value of PSNR, the better the visual quality of the stego, and the less the chances of detecting the hidden message [16, 17].

9.4 Conclusion

The proposed technique demonstrates significant potential for secure information concealment in the digital era. The authors have employed a dual-key mechanism for embedding and retrieving secret data using LSB steganography. Although managing two keys introduces complexity, it substantially enhances the security of the concealed information. The results validate the technique's effectiveness, as the presence of hidden data remains imperceptible to unauthorized parties. Incorporating two secret keys introduces a high degree of randomness into the steganography process, making it highly challenging for an intruder to detect or extract the hidden content without access to the keys. Furthermore, the high PSNR value achieved confirms that the visual quality of the stego file remains intact, thereby reducing the likelihood of suspicion or detection by third parties.

References

[1] Jebur, S. A., Nawar, A. K., Kadhim, L. E., & Jahefer, M. M. (2023). Hiding information in digital images using the LSB steganography technique. *International Journal of Interactive Mobile Technologies, 17*(7), 167–178.

[2] Rafat, K. F., & Sajjad, S. M. (2024). Advancing reversible LSB steganography: Addressing imperfections and embracing pioneering techniques for enhanced security. *IEEE Access*.

[3] Dumre, R., & Dave, A. (2021, July). Exploring LSB steganography possibilities in RGB images. In *2021, the 12th International Conference on Computing, Communication, and Networking Technologies* (pp. 1–7). IEEE.

[4] Tiwari, K., & Gangurde, S. J. (2021, May). LSB steganography using pixel locator sequence with AES. In *2021 2nd International Conference on Secure Cyber Computing and Communications* (pp. 302–307). IEEE.

[5] Njoum, M., Sulaiman, R., Shukur, Z., & Qamar, F. (2024). High-secured image LSB steganography using AVL-Tree with random RGB channel substitution. *Computers, Materials & Continua, 81*(1), 183–210.

[6] Srinidhi, S. K., Vishal, K. S., Shashank, U. S., Prabhakar, T. N., & Singh, R. (2024, October). Video based steganography for audio using lsb approach. In *2024 IEEE International Conference on Computer Vision and Machine Intelligence* (pp. 1–6). IEEE.

[7] Kumar, N., Lakhani, V., Singh, K., Bhardwaj, M., & Raj, S. (2024, March). Development of LSB based steganography method for video and image hiding. In *2024 11th International Conference on Reliability, Infocom Technologies and Optimization (Trends and Future Directions)* (pp. 1–6). IEEE.

[8] Kobozieva, A., Bobok, I., & Kushnirenko, N. (2023). Steganalysis method for detecting LSB embedding in digital video, digital image sequence. In: *ICST-2023: Information Control Systems & Technologies, September 21-23, 2023, Odesa, Ukraine, Publication detail- CEUR Workshop Proceedings* (pp. 78–90).

[9] Chuang, Y. H., Lin, B. S., Chen, Y. X., & Shiu, H. J. (2021). Steganography in RGB images using adjacent mean. *IEEE access*, *9*, 164256–164274.

[10] Patel, R., Lad, K., & Patel, M. (2022). Novel DCT and DST based video steganography algorithms over non-dynamic region in compressed domain: A comparative analysis. *International Journal of Information Technology*, *14*(3), 1649–1657.

[11] Prasad, S., Pal, A. K., & Mukherjee, S. (2023). An RGB color image steganography scheme by binary lower triangular matrix. *IEEE Transactions on Intelligent Transportation Systems*, *24*(7), 6865–6873.

[12] Bunyamin, R. F., D'Layla, A. W. C., De La Croix, N. J., & Ahmad, T. (2024, December). Adaptive steganography approach in RGBiImages based on color channels to enhance stego image quality. In *2024 IEEE 16th International Conference on Computational Intelligence and Communication Networks* (pp. 542–546). IEEE.

[13] Podile, N., Ahmed, M. S., Nalajala, V., Kodali, M. H., & Kukunuri, Y. S. M. (2025). Secure and robust data hiding in RGB images using steganography. *International Journal on Science and Technology*, *16*(2), 1–13.

[14] Takaoğlu, M., Özyavaş, A., Ajlouni, N., & Takaoğlu, F. (2023). Highly secured hybrid image steganography with an improved key generation and exchange for one-time-pad encryption method. *Afyon Kocatepe Üniversitesi Fen Ve Mühendislik Bilimleri Dergisi*, *23*(1), 101–114.

[15] Vhito, K., & Chouvatut, V. (2023, June). Steganography with adaptable separate encrypted code of hidden confidential information. In *2023 20th International Joint Conference on Computer Science and Software Engineering (JCSSE)* (pp. 523–528). IEEE.

[16] Pilania, U., Kumar, M., Singh, S., & Mittal, V. (2023, June). Video steganography in IoT: Information embedding using OpenCV and 2LSB. In *2023 International Conference on Sustainable Computing and Smart Systems* (pp. 1067–1072). IEEE.

[17] Pilania, U., Kumar, M., & Mittal, V. (2023). Performance evaluation of LSB steganography based on multiple image formats. *Journal of Discrete Mathematical Sciences and Cryptography*, *26*(7), 1911–1924.

10

A Novel Approach for Design and Implementation of Optimized Robust High-Capacity Video Steganography

10.1 Introduction

Network security is a subset of cybersecurity. Network security protects secret information in transmission, but cybersecurity protects digital data from all threats. Both network and cybersecurity provide confidentiality, authentication, and integrity of hidden details. The network security system is divided into information encryption and information embedding techniques. Information encryption includes cryptography, whereas information embedding includes watermarking and steganography [1]. The objective of cryptography is secret writing, whereas watermarking aims to verify, identify, and authenticate the user [2]. Steganography is the concealment of secret data inside a carrier file. The hidden secret information is then stored and forwarded to the destination without the third party's knowledge [3].

Nowadays, everyone uses digital steganography most commonly. It uses text, images, audio, video, and protocols to hide secret information [4]. Text steganography is the most straightforward technique with low concealing capacity and poor imperceptibility. The security of this technique can be improved by using a secret key. It causes problems with redrafting, altering the line's texture, and accumulation or elimination of words. Image steganography is more prevalent than

DOI: 10.1201/9781003504139-10

text steganography regarding safety and information hiding capacity [5]. In it, concealing secret data is unnoticeable by making a minor alteration to the color values of an image. For the safety of secret data, additional padding is required around the secret data. Audio steganography examines inaudible frequencies for embedding secret data. In this research work, video steganography is chosen to embed secret information. Some essential features of video steganography explain the need for video cover files over other multimedia files [6, 7]:

- Because of their large size, video cover files have a high-concealing capacity.
- Video can be decomposed into multiple frames through images and inaudible frequencies. Then these frames can be used to embed the secret information randomly.
- Multiple frames can be used to embed the secret data. Embedding secret information into multiple frames creates difficulty for hackers in detecting the secret information.
- The first challenge for the hacker is to identify the number of frames where secret information is embedded. The second challenge is to retrieve the embedded secret data.
- Because of the dynamic nature of the video, the probability of noticing embedded secret data is much lower than in still images and inaudible frequencies.

The proposed work combines the features of OpenCV, JPEG, and IWT techniques. The features of the mentioned techniques for improving the proposed research work's performance are as follows: OpenCV is compatible with many programming languages. The OpenCV library is freely available for platforms such as Windows, iOS, Android, Linux, and many more. This library supports computer vision, image processing, and machine learning algorithms. OpenCV helps to find the region of interest for hiding secret data. Hiding secret data in the area of interest improves the imperceptibility of the work. JPEG works efficiently with large files and complex images. It allows up to 95% compression of the original file. JPEG compression is compatible with almost all image-processing techniques. It can store and forward data in efficient ways. It helps improve the concealing capacity of the proposed work by reducing the size of the secret message.

IWT provides in-place calculation, resulting in less memory usage. It performs operations on integer numbers faster than other traditional techniques. As IWT works on integer numbers, the signal reconstruction is lossless. Because of its integer nature, this technique takes significantly less power to compute the input signal. Due to all the mentioned properties, it provides optimized computational overhead for the proposed work.

This chapter is organized into eight sections. Section 10.1 describes the introduction of the proposed technique. Section 10.2 has a literature review of the latest steganography techniques, and challenges are listed as points. In Section 10.3, all the performance metrics are clarified through equations. In Section 10.4, the motivation for the proposed work, along with the problem statement, is specified. In section 10.5, the work plan and methodology are explained with the help of secret information concealing and retrieval flowcharts at the receiver end. In section 10.6, result analysis has been done on the following parameters: Imperceptibility analysis, concealing and retrieval capacity analysis, robustness-against-attacks analysis, and computational overhead analysis. A comparison of the work is also done with the state-of-the-art methods in Section 10.7. Finally, in section 10.8, the proposed work is concluded along with the future scope.

10.2 Literature Review

In the research work, JPEG steganography was performed to decrease the distortion caused by hiding secret information. The author focused on feature distortion to avoid steganalysis attacks. The JPEG image was converted into a reference image with almost the same quality. The LSB technique was applied to embed secret data. Information embedding is simple and easy using the LSB techniques. The stego was robust against steganalysis tools. The proposed work carries a low embedding capacity. On embedding, a large amount of secret data quality of the stego file degrades [8].To enhance concealing capacity, other parameters of the magic triangle were compromised. So, in the next research work, the author used the DCT to embed secret information. DCT-based techniques work in the transform domain, and these techniques can embed a large amount of information without degrading the visual quality of the stego file. The author calculated modulus three and then found the difference between two DCT variables to embed the secret information. JPEG compression was used to decrease the size of the stego to the original file. Because of the embedding process, there was a slight change in the statistical properties of the cover file. The proposed work's embedding capacity was improved compared to the previous work. Embedding capacity was calculated as 17% of the cover file [9].

In almost all online communication applications, encryption is used to provide security. In some cases, steganography is also used to improve the security level. A reversible data-hiding approach was used to embed secret information. The cover file was taken as JPEG images. The hidden information was transformed into binary form before actual embedding. The nonzero coefficients were used to embed data, resulting in high embedding capacity. Histograms were drawn for the original and the stego file to analyze experimental results. The proposed technique was suitable for low-bandwidth communication. In the case of high bandwidth, the stego file was not robust against different image-processing attacks [10]. Transform-domain-based steganography techniques first work on the Region of Interest (ROI) for embedding information. These techniques are robust against image-processing attacks such as clipping, cropping, translation, rotation, and others. In the proposed research work, SVD, along with IWT), was combined to enhance the visual quality of the stego file. Actual embedding was done through IWT, and compression was done using the SVD technique. A histogram was drawn to check the quality of the research work [11].

These days, people of all age groups use the Internet for communication. So, information safety has become a significant challenge in online transmission. Many researchers and academicians are already working to resolve the challenges. The authors propose the chaotic map-based spatial-domain steganography technique in this paper. Three variables were used to calculate the positions of pixels in the cover file using the chaotic map. Chaotic maps are very sensitive to even slight changes. For the analysis of the work, some image-processing attacks were chosen. A Stego file is robust against attacks but carries low embedding capacity [12]. Watermarking also provides security against copyright protection and authentication in multimedia files.

The authors proposed the DWT and SVD in the transform domain in this work. RGB images were first converted into YCbCr format, and then DWT was applied to different blocks to embed the secret information. The stego file carries almost no distortion and is robust against attacks. Robustness was checked using compression attacks, geometric attacks, gamma-correlation attacks, etc. [13].

The authors worked on multimodal steganography and visual cryptography in the proposed work. The authors calculated PSNR ∞ to hide data using multimodal steganography. A PSNR value of 51 is achieved against a salt-and-pepper attack. The authors used the Viola–Jones algorithm and the rotation-bit operator to find the ROI. Using a multimodal mask, biometric features are extracted to hide the secret data. Cryptography adds more security to the proposed technique by encrypting the secret message. PSNR, MSE, CC, SSIM, and attacks were used to check the performance of the work [14]. The author proposed image steganography for underwater acoustic communication using IWT and Particle Swarm Optimization (PSO) in this work. The first authors studied underwater images to hide secret messages and enhance the detection and regeneration of the cover image. The input cover image is divided into blocks to hide the secret message, and IWT is used on each block. Doing so minimized the PSO search space to optimize the technique's performance. At last, communication error, revealing, and retrieval processes were applied to the retrieved secret message to enhance reconstruction quality. The results of the proposed work proved that the proposed work has better hiding capacity and visual quality of the stego file [15].

High concealing capacity, good visual quality, and robustness against attacks are the main concerns in steganography techniques. The authors tried their best to achieve high concealing capacity and imperceptibility in the proposed work. The authors proposed an image steganography technique using IWT and diamond encoding. To fulfill the above objective, the authors utilized all the redundant bits of the cover file to minimize distortion. IWT can efficiently divide the input image into the frequency domain. Diamond encoding was used to find the suitable region of interest. The developed technique achieved a good concealing capacity, robustness against attacks, better visual quality of the stego file, and a PSNR value of 65.46 dB [16].

Video cover files are large in size and dynamic in nature. The large size of the video results in good concealing capacity and high security. The authors proposed H.264 video steganography using Quantized Discrete Cosine Transform (QDCT). QDCT coefficients depend on the neighbor block coefficients. Modifying any of the coefficients in a block affects all the adjacent blocks. After embedding secret information, the stego file was compressed using the JPEG compression method. The quality of research work was analyzed through different performance metrics [17]. To obtain the magic triangle, the author of this paper proposed a new steganography technique using the transform domain. The HH coefficients were extracted from the frame, and then secret information was embedded. As the HH coefficient carries the least significant data, it can be used to embed hidden information. JPEG compression was performed to ensure the robustness of the work. The proposed work was found to be flexible, as changing some parameters, its performance varies in capacity and imperceptibility [18]. After a literature survey of papers from 2008 to 2022, the challenges are listed as follows:

- A trade-off exists between the magic triangle's three sides, i.e., concealing capacity, imperceptibility, and robustness.
- Many traditional steganography techniques exist, such as DCT, DWT, DFT, LSB, and MSB. All the mentioned techniques generate floating-point coefficients, resulting in a loss of information.
- A suitable compression technique is required to improve the embedding capacity.
- Computational overhead increases because of the hybrid techniques, so optimization needs to be done in time and space.
- In the case of a video as a cover file, one needs to calculate a suitable region of interest for embedding secret information.

10.3 Measures of Steganography Techniques

The excellence of steganography techniques is measured as computational overhead, capacity, robustness, and imperceptibility [19]. Capacity is the amount of secret data concealed in the carrier file. Robustness is the capability of hidden secret information to remain unchanged and unharmed even if the stego file is exposed to various image-processing attacks. Imperceptibility stands for the visibility of exchange inside the carrier file. High imperceptibility means it is difficult to detect the embedded secret information. Capacity, imperceptibility, and robustness are the three sides of the magic triangle. On the increase, anyone on one side was automatically affected; it is also evident from the literature review. One parameter of the magic triangle can be achieved easily, but when one focuses on the combination of parameters, the problem arises. The magic triangle's objective is to balance data hiding capacity and robustness properly while preserving the stego file's video quality.

Table 10.1 lists performance metrics MSE, PSNR, SSIM, and CC as Equations 1, 2, 3, and 4, respectively. PSNR, SSIM, CC, MSE, and image-processing attack scans are used to find the acceptable value of security, robustness, and imperceptibility. PSNR value above '35' represents good quality of the stego file, which means the stego file is robust against attacks [22]. Values of performance metrics: MSE, SSIM, and CC vary from '0' to '1'. Value '1' of performance metric: SSIM and CC represent the stego file's good quality and robustness against attacks. Different attacks can be applied to the stego file to check robustness and expose hidden secret data.

10.4 Motivation and Problem Statement

The motivation for the work is to achieve all three parameters of the magic triangle: high embedding capacity, robustness against attacks, and imperceptibility. A video is chosen as the carrier file to increase the embedding capacity. Video is converted into several frames and an inaudible frequency. So, the user has the option of embedding secret information in frames as well as inaudible frequencies. Secret information can be embedded randomly into more than one frame; randomness will result in more security. JPEG compression is applied to the hidden information to reduce its size, enhancing the concealing capacity. To achieve high imperceptibility and robustness against attacks, a suitable ROI is chosen from the cover video file using OpenCV. A hybrid of the mentioned two techniques improves embedding capacity, imperceptibility, and robustness, but at the same time, the computational

Table 10.1 Performance Metrics

MSE stands for Mean Squared Error. It measures the error present in the stego file by comparing it with the original cover file [20].	$MSE = \frac{1}{n}\sum_{i=0}^{i=n}\left[I(i) - J(i)\right]^2$	(1)	I(i) is the input file, and J(i) is the generated stego file.
It finds the ratio of noise present between the original and the stego image [21].	$PSNR = 10\log_{10}\left(\frac{MAX_I^2}{MSE}\right)$	(2)	MAXI is the maximum possible power of the signal. Its value varies from 0 to 255. MSE represents the power of the corrupted signal.
SSIM stands for Structure Similarity Index Metric. It works on the structure of the input and stego files. It performs better than PSNR and MSE [22].	$\mathrm{SSIM}(x,y) = \left[l(x,y)^{\alpha} \times c(x,y)^{\beta} \times s(x,y)^{\gamma}\right]$	(3)	Here, l represents luminance, c contrast, and s structure. α, β, and γ are the constants. Generally, the value of these constants is taken as 1 for good results.
The correlation coefficient (CC) is the statistical measurement of the relationship between two variables showing a linear connection [23, 24].	$r_{xy} = \frac{\Sigma\left(X_i - \bar{X}\right)\left(Y_i - \bar{Y}\right)}{\sqrt{\Sigma\left(X_i - \bar{X}\right)^2 \Sigma\left(Y_i - \bar{Y}\right)^2}}$	(4)	Where Xi and Yi are variables in the input sample, rxy- represents the correlation coefficient, $\bar{x}$- mean of variable Xi, $\bar{y}$- mean of variable Yi.

overhead will increase. So, to overcome computational overhead, IWT is chosen for the actual embedding process. IWT performs in-place computation on integer numbers, so there is no requirement for secondary memory. It can also reconstruct the original signal because of its integer nature.

Based on the challenges in the literature review, a problem statement has been designed and developed. The video steganography technique is created through appropriate optimization steps, which are robust against attacks. It carries high concealing capacity with the decent visual quality of a stego file while maintaining computational overhead. The primary focus of the problem statement is to obtain the magic triangle with low computational overhead.

10.5 Work Plan and Methodology

The proposed hybrid video steganography technique focuses on achieving the magic triangle with low computational overhead—video as a cover file helps to improve the embedding capacity and imperceptibility. Randomly concealed secret data enhances the security of the proposed technique. The size of the secret image is first reduced using JPEG compression, resulting in high embedding capacity. Hiding secret data in the face of the frame results in high robustness, as the human face has a maximum of valuable data in the low-frequency components, so high-frequency components can be used to conceal the secret message. The frames carrying the face are detected by using the OpenCV library. Finally, IWT is applied to optimize the computational overhead. The hidden information concealing and extraction process is explained with the help of flowcharts.

10.5.1 Concealing Process

Input is taken as the carrier video file and the secret image. After concealing secret information, output is produced as a stego video. OpenCV detects faces from the cover video, which acts as the region of interest for hiding secret information. JPEG compression is used to reduce the size of the image and improve embedding capacity. JPEG is compatible with working on the hybrid technique. We have chosen a video as a cover file, and JPEG works efficiently with complex files. It can store and forward data in a short time [25]. IWT is applied to calculate the ROI's HH, LL, LH, and HL coefficients. The total length of the compressed secret image is concealed inside the HH coefficients using the wavelet domain. In this way, the stego file is created. The Stego file has now been sent to the recipient. At the destination, the receiver applies inverse IWT to retrieve the secret image from the output file.

Figure 10.1 represents the stepwise flow of the research work. The iteration is used for the secret image and cover file. Iteration in the case of secret information checks whether complete data is concealed. Iteration in the cover file finds the next frame for concealing secret information. The process will repeat until complete secret data is not hidden in the carrier file.

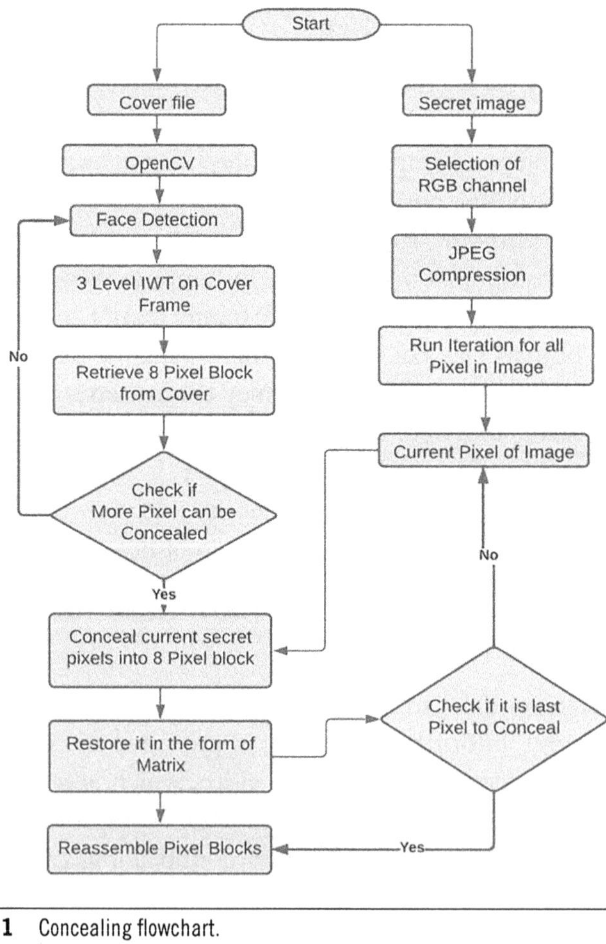

Figure 10.1 Concealing flowchart.

10.5.2 Retrieval Process

A reverse process must be carried out during the retrieval of secret information from the stego file, as shown in Figure 10.2. Iteration is applied to retrieve complete secret information. The retrieved secret image is then returned to its original form using the reverse JPEG compression technique. All the extracted frames are combined to create an original video.

The input cover video, secret image, and stego video may undergo several adjustments during acquisition, dispensation, loading, storage, transmission, and imitation. Because of image-processing techniques, the visual quality of input and output images may be compromised. The decisive objective of this work is to design and develop a hybrid video steganography technique that can achieve all the parameters of the magic triangle. The developed and designed technique must have its application in the real-life online transmission of secret data.

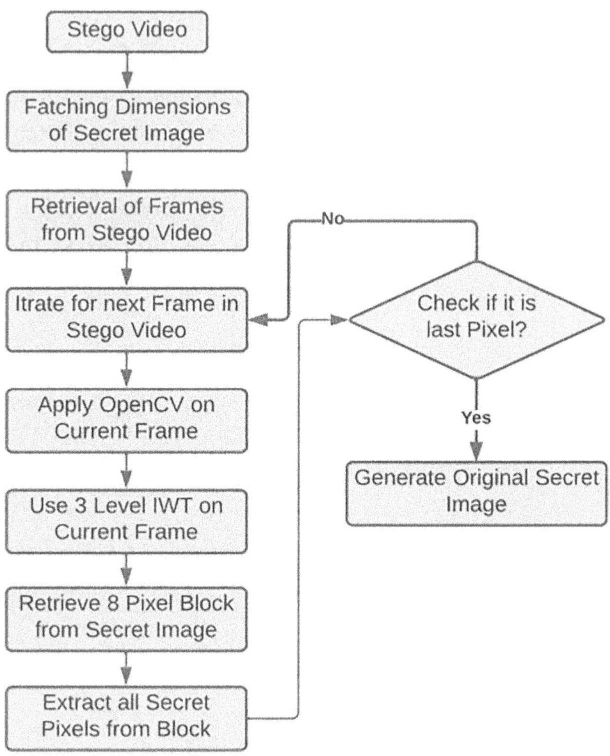

Figure 10.2 Retrieval flowchart.

10.6 Experimental Results and Analysis

The hybrid video steganography technique is designed and developed in this research work to improve the security level during information communication. The experiment is conducted in MATLAB to analyze and validate the research work. For the experiment, secret information is taken as an image, and three videos as a cover file. The effectiveness of research work is calculated based on imperceptibility analysis, embedding capacity analysis, robustness analysis, and computational-overhead analysis.

10.6.1 Imperceptibility Analysis

Imperceptibility means the invisibility of hidden exchange during transmission. The higher the imperceptibility, the lower the probability of exposure to hidden secret messages. Imperceptibility can be measured by checking the statistical properties of the original and stego frames. The change in the statistical values detects the presence of hidden exchange. PSNR, MSE, SSIM, and CC values are computed for both the original and stego files to check imperceptibility. Figure 10.3 displays performance metrics for the stego file.

Three cover videos are taken to validate and compare the experimental results for imperceptibility. '1' is the highest value for MSE, SSIM, and CC performance metrics. In the case of SSIM and CC,

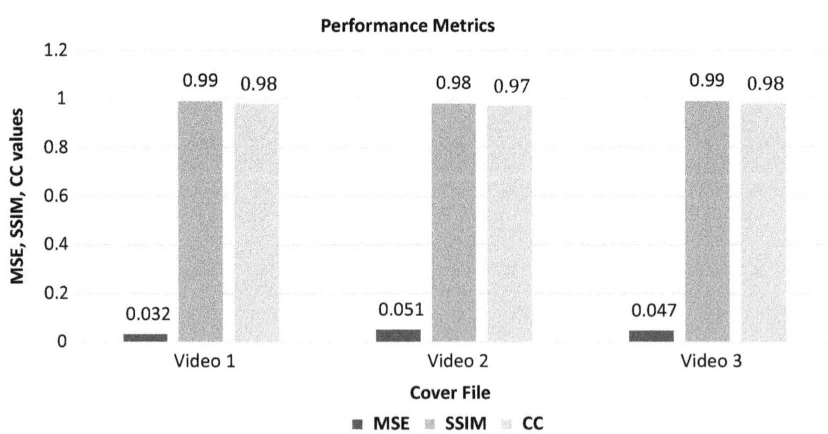

Figure 10.3 Imperceptibility analysis of stego file.

'1' means the stego file seems to be a copy of the original cover file. In the case of MSE, '1' indicates the worst quality of the stego file and the highest chance of detecting secret data. Lowering the MSE value means less alteration between the original and stego file. PSNR value greater than 35 represents a good quality stego file and fewer chances of exposure of the secret message [22]. The average PSNR value is calculated at 67 dB for the proposed research work. The average SSIM is estimated at 0.99, representing the work's high imperceptibility. The average CC is calculated at 0.98 for the job, which is also considered proof of high imperceptibility.

10.6.2 Embedding-Capacity Analysis

Embedding capacity is the amount of secret information that can be concealed without degradation in the visual quality of the carrier file. Cover video is decomposed into the number of images and inaudible frequency frames. The user can hide secret information in either photos or inaudible frequencies. In the case of video files, many options are available to conceal secret messages, resulting in enhanced security. The dynamic nature of video reduces the chances of detecting hidden secret information. The size of the video can be found by using Equation 10.1.

$$Size\,of\,Video = T'F'P'B \tag{10.1}$$

Where T is the entire time of the video in seconds, F is the number of frames per second, P is the number of pixels per frame, and D is the bit depth. The size of the secret image can be calculated with Equation 10.2.

$$Image\,Size = V'H'CD \tag{10.2}$$

V is the image's vertical resolution, H is the horizontal resolution of the image, and CD is the color depth for the input image. The embedding capacity for the research work can be calculated by Equation 10.3 for the region of interest.

$$Embedding\,Capacity\,for\,ROI = (N \times F)/Fs \tag{10.3}$$

Where N represents the altered bits concealed in the region of interest of a particular frame, F is the frame rate in seconds, and Fs

Table 10.2 Embedding Capacity Analysis

COVER VIDEO	FRAME SIZE	NUMBER OF FRAMES	FRAME RATE	CAPACITY
Video 1	180×185	3200	26	38
Video 2	190×185	3186	30	35
Video3	170×190	3063	28	39

represents the frame size in height and width. Table 10.2 represents the hiding capacity of the video cover file in the region of interest for the research work.

For the research work, embedding capacity is calculated to be approximately 37.33 bps. The videos are chosen with varying properties such as different frame sizes, numbers of frames per second, frame rates, etc. Videos are taken in .mp4 format for the work. The varying conditions of the cover videos do not affect the embedding capacity. Varying conditions for the cover video files represent the reliability of the proposed work. The proposed work is reliable and applicable to different types of cover video files.

10.6.3 Robustness Analysis

Robustness means the undetectability of hidden information even when exposed to different image-processing attacks. To check robustness, the following attacks are tried on the stego file: salt-and-pepper and cropping attacks. After applying attacks on the stego file, the performance metrics are calculated. The acceptable values of performance metrics show the robustness of the research work. All the mentioned attacks are explained one by one with their screenshots and performance metrics as follows:

10.6.3.1 Salt-and-Pepper Attack In this attack, some noise is added to the input file to check the robustness of the work. The noise is generated because of the unexpected and strident disorder in the input image. Defective camera sensors may result in salt and pepper noise. The added noise is presented in the form of white and black dots. It is a very effective attack for checking the robustness. Noise added in the form of salt and pepper attacks degrades the image quality, resulting in data loss. It affects only some pixels of the input file, but not all the pixels. Pepper-to-salt noise intensity values vary from 0 to 255. Low-, medium-, and high-pass filtering can be used to reduce the effect of this attack.

$$p(z) = \begin{Bmatrix} p_a & z = a \\ p_b & z = b \\ 0 & Otherwise \end{Bmatrix} \tag{10.4}$$

Equation 10.4 represents the salt-and-pepper attack. If b>a, a light dot will appear; dark dots will also generate noise in the input image. Pa = pb = 0 means unipolar; $p_a \approx p_b$ then salt and pepper will appear, and p (z) represents the probability density function.

Table 10.3 shows the salt-and-pepper attack with varying noise densities. Three videos are taken as the cover file, having different properties. One by one, the same secret image "Lena" is hidden in video frames with a noise density of 0.01, 0.05, and 0.1. On the increasing Density of noise quality of the stego frame, the secret image is retrieved, and the cover image degrades.

Table 10.4 represents the quality of the stego file based on various performance metrics after applying the salt-and-pepper attack. The quality of stego degrades with a higher degree of the noise density function. The average PSNR value for salt-and-pepper attack is 45.5, the average MSE is 0.62, the average SSIM is 0.98, and the average CC is 0.98.

10.6.3.2 Cropping Attack Cropping is a type of geometric attack. In geometric attacks, geometric distortions are applied to the input image to expose the hidden secret data. Generally, cropping is defined as the removal of the unwanted outer area from the input image. However, cropping can be done on any part of the image to check the robustness of the work. Sometimes, cropping source images may affect hidden secret information.

Table 10.5 represents the cropping effect with different percentage values of cropping, which are 20, 30, and 40. Three videos are taken to visualize the impact of a cropping attack or to check the robustness of the stego file. With an increasing percentage of cropping attack quality of the stego file, the retrieved secret image degrades, and hidden information loss is also present.

Table 10.3 Salt-and-Pepper Attack with varying Density

	DENSITY	VIDEO COVER FRAME	SECRET IMAGE	STEGO FRAME	RETRIEVED SECRET IMAGE	RETRIEVED COVER FRAME
Salt-and-Pepper Attack	0.01	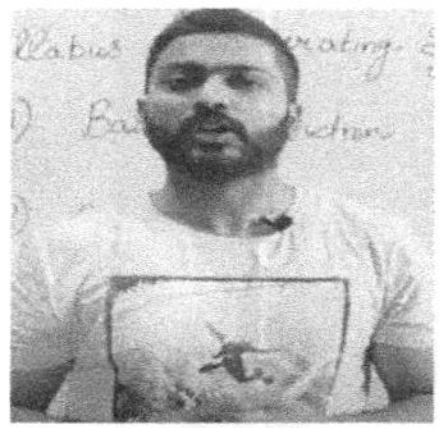				
	0.05					
	0.1					

Table 10.4 Performance Metrics for Salt-and-Pepper Attack

	ATTACK DENSITY	PSNR	MSE	SSIM	CC
	0.01	47.1	0.56	0.989	0.987
SALT AND PEPPER	0.05	45.3	0.62	0.983	0.984
ATTACK	0.10	44.1	0.69	0.978	0.981

Table 10.6 shows the values of the stego file for performance metrics with varying percentages of cropping attacks. From the experiment, it was determined that the value of the stego file and information loss occurred due to the cropping attack. The average PSNR value is 25.6 dB, the average MSE is 4.65, the average SSIM is 0.59, and the average CC is 0.97.

10.6.4 *Computation-Overhead Analysis*

Computational overhead is defined regarding concealing and retrieval time for the proposed research work. In real-life applications, computational overhead plays an important role. The concealing and retrieval time varies with the cover video's size and format. It is also contingent on the format and size of the secret message. IWT is chosen for the actual concealing and retrieval of hidden information. Because of many good features of IWT over the traditional DWT technique, it provides lower computational overhead. IWT performs in-place computation and works on integer numbers, thus diminishing computational overhead. It can reform the signals without any loss of data. As it works in both time and frequency domains, it can easily analyze discontinuities and sharp spikes in the signal. IWT also avoids smoothing the main features of the input signal, resulting in good speed.

$$Embedding\ time = \frac{Secret\ Data\ Size \times Video\ Frames}{\cdots} \tag{10.5}$$

Equation 10.5 represents the embedding time for the secret information. Secret data embedding time is required to embed secret data in the number of video frames in a fixed time interval. Hiding secret data randomly in a huge number of frames enhances the security of confidential data, but the time complexity increases.

Table 10.5 Cropping Attack with varying Percentage

		VIDEO COVER FRAME	SECRET IMAGE	STEGO FRAME	RETRIEVED SECRET IMAGE	RETRIEVED COVER FRAME
Cropping Attack	20			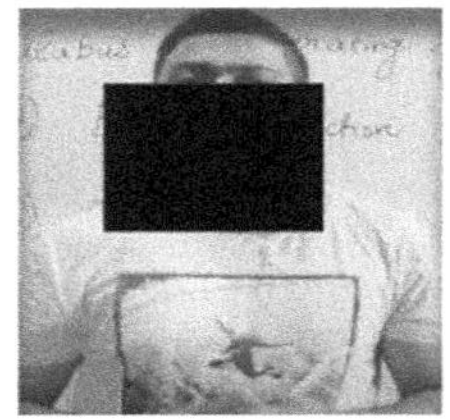	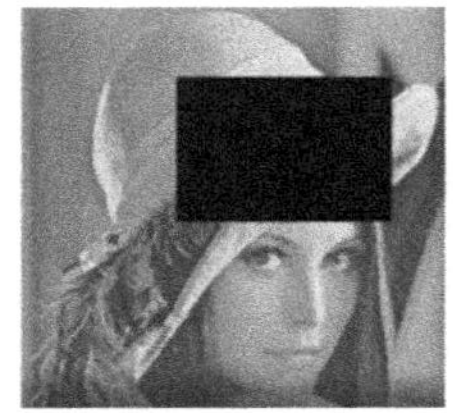	
	30			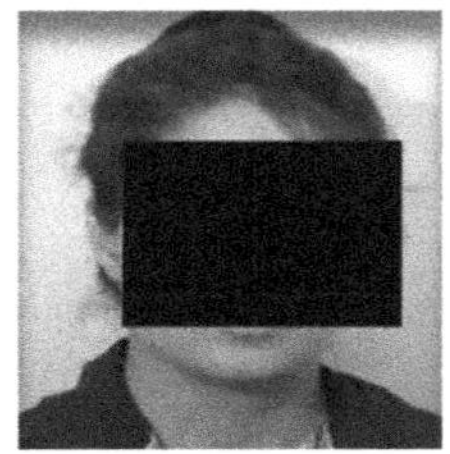		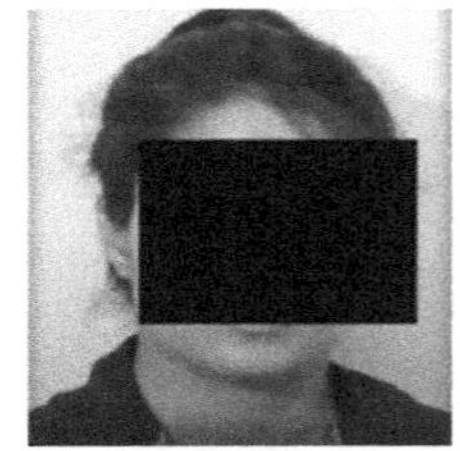
	40			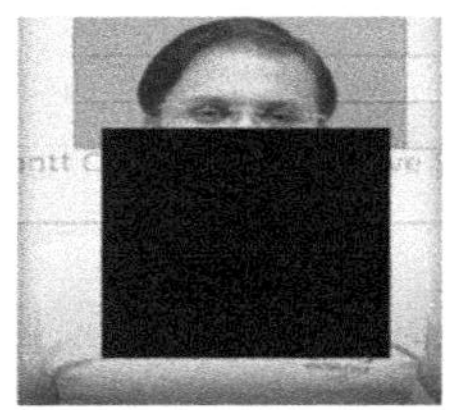		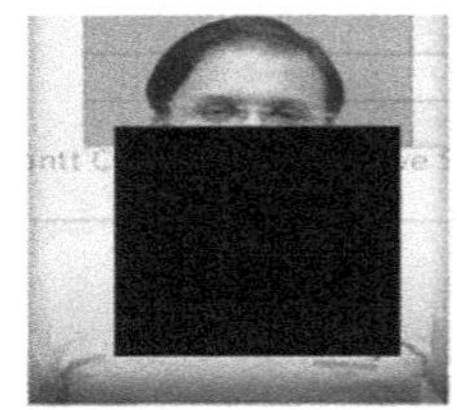

Table 10.6 Performance Metrics for Cropping Attack

	CROPPING %	PSNR	MSE	SSIM	CC
	20	30.1	2.02	0.74	0.987
	30	26.3	4.52	0.61	0.977
CROPPING ATTACK	40	21.5	7.43	0.42	0.967

Table 10.7 Computational Analysis

COVER FILE	SECRET IMAGE	CONCEALING TIME	RETRIEVAL TIME
Video 1	Lena Image	0.582	0.352
Video 2	Lena Image	0.643	0.403
Video 3	Lena Image	0.611	0.389

$$Retrieval\ Time \frac{= Retrieved\ Secret\ Data}{Time \times Video\ Frames} \tag{10.6}$$

Equation 10.6 represents the amount of time needed to embed the secret message. Retrieval time depends on how many frames are used to hide the data; as the number of frames increases, retrieval time increases, but results in more security.

Table 10.7 represents the computational overhead for the three different cover videos. From the experimental results, the minimum concealing time is 0.582 s, and the minimum retrieval time is 0.352 s for the .mp4 video format. The IWT technique reduced the computational overhead because of simple algebraic manipulations.

10.7 Comparison

The proposed research work is compared and analyzed with three existing similar research articles [26, 27, 28]. The analysis is done based on performance metrics: MSE, PSNR, SSIM, concealing capacity, concealing time, and retrieval time. The existing techniques are robust and carry good visual quality in the experimental results.

Figure 10.4 compares the proposed technique to three existing state-of-the-art methods. The comparison is based on concealing capacity, PSNR, MSE, SSIM, and total time for hiding and retrieving secret data. The comparison of the proposed work is as follows:

- Concealing capacity is calculated at 37 bps for the work, which is much better than the state of the artwork.

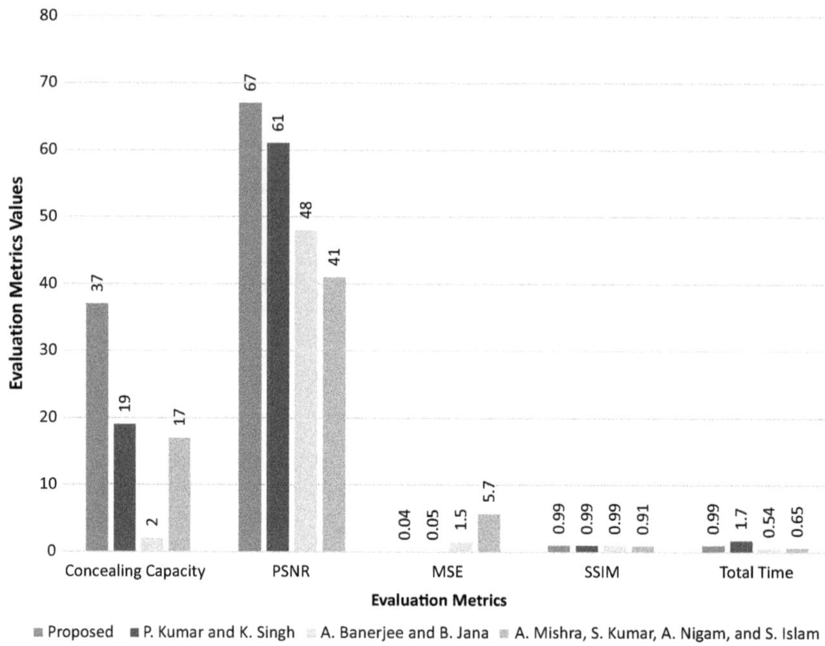

Figure 10.4 Comparison of proposed technique with existing techniques.

- PSNR value came out to be 67dB for the proposed work. PSNR value represents the visual quality of the stego file. The higher the PSNR value, the lower the chances of detection of secret information.
- Although the concealing time for the work is highest compared to the state-of-the-art techniques, concealing time increased for the job because we have concealed a large amount of secret data compared to the mentioned techniques.
- MSE value is calculated approximately equal to '0' for the work. Paper [26] also has an almost '0' MSE value, but other metrics for the proposed work performed better than [26].
- We have achieved good concealing capacity through appropriate optimization steps with decent visual quality of the stego file while maintaining computational overhead.
- The comparison results witness the improved performance of the research work.

10.8 Conclusion

From the literature review, it has been concluded that a trade-off exists between concealing capacity, imperceptibility, robustness, and computational overhead. OpenCV provided a suitable ROI for embedding secret data in the cover video file, JPEG compression provided improved concealing capacity by reducing the size of secret information before concealing, and IWT optimized the computational overhead in terms of concealing and retrieval time because of its integer nature. PSNR, SSIM, MSE, and CC performance metrics were used to check imperceptibility. Attacks such as salt-and-pepper and cropping are applied to analyze robustness. The computational overhead is determined in terms of concealing capacity and retrieval time. Concealing capacity is measured in BPS. Research results support the achievement of the proposed research work, which is laid out primarily. The comparison results witness the improved performance of the research work.

With the growth of online-transmission techniques, data security during communication has become more difficult. The huge gap between the skill set of unofficial and civic users' needs secure data communication which is very inspirational as well as challenging. The proposed research work can be further extended by using some authentication process, which results in improved security of the technique.

References

[1] Pilania, U., Tanwar, R., & Gupta, P. (2021). Stable high capacity video steganography in wavelet domain. *Turkish Journal of Computer and Mathematics Education Research Article*, *12*(7), 2142–2158.

[2] Chang, K. C., Chang, C. P., Huang, P. S., & Tu, T. M. (2008). A novel image steganographic method using tri-way pixel-value differencing. *Journal of Multimedia*, *3*(2), 37–44.

[3] Xie, P., Zhang, H., You, W., Zhao, X., Yu, J., & Ma, Y. (2019). Adaptive VP8 steganography based on deblocking filtering. In *Proceedings of the ACM Workshop on Information Hiding and Multimedia Security (IH MMSec 2019)* (pp. 25–30).

[4] Shanthakumari, R., & Malliga, D. (2014). Video steganography using lsb matching revisited algorithm. *IOSR Journal Computer Engineering*, *16*(6), 1–6.

[5] Pilania, U., & Gupta, P. (2019). A proposed optimized steganography technique using ROI, IWT and SVD. *International Journal of Information Systems & Management Science*, 313–318.

[6] Mukherjee (Ganguly), N., Paul, G., & Saha, S. K. (2018). An efficient multi-bit steganography algorithm in spatial domain with two-layer security. *Multimedia Tools and Applications*, *77*(14), 18451–18481.
[7] Pilania, U., Tanwar, R., & Gupta, P. (2022). An ROI-based robust video steganography technique using SVD in the wavelet domain. *Open Computer Science*, *12*(1), 1–16.
[8] Wang, Z., Qian, Z., Zhang, X., Yang, M., & Ye, D. (2018). On improving distortion functions for JPEG steganography. *IEEE Access*, *6*, 74917–74930.
[9] Attaby, A. A., Mursi Ahmed, M. F. M., & Alsammak, A. K. (2018). Data hiding inside JPEG images with high resistance to steganalysis using a novel technique: DCT-M3. *Ain Shams Engineering Journal*, 9(4), 1965–1974.
[10] Liu, Y., & Chang, C. C. (2018). Reversible data hiding for JPEG images employing all quantized non-zero AC coefficients. *Displays*, *51*(1), 51–56.
[11] Singh, S., Singh, R., & Siddiqui, T. J. (2016). Singular value decomposition based image steganography using integer wavelet transform. *Advances in Intelligent Systems and Computing*, 425, 593–601.
[12] Valandar, M. Y., Ayubi, P., & Barani, M. J. (2015). High secure digital image steganography based on 3D chaotic map. In *2015 7th Conference on Information & Knowledge Technology* (pp. 1–6). IEEE. https://doi.org/10.1109/IKT.2015.7288810
[13] Roy, S., & Pal, A. K. (2019). A hybrid domain color image watermarking based on DWT–SVD. *Iran Journal of Science and Technology – Transactions of Electrical Engineering*, *43*(2), 201–217.
[14] Jahnavi, S., & Nandini, C. (2022). Secure two-fold transmission of features using multimodal mask steganography and naive-based random visual cryptography system. *International Journal of System Assurance Engineering and Management*. https://doi.org/10.1007/s13198-022-01701-6
[15] Wang, W., & Li, Q. (2022). An image steganography algorithm based on PSO and IWT for underwater acoustic communication. *IEEE Access*, *10*(1), 107376–107385.
[16] Idakwo, M. A., Mu'azu, M. B., Adedokun, E. A., & Sadiq, B. O. (2022). Development of a non-separable integer-to-integer wavelet transform-based digital image steganography system. *Model*, *6*, 20–27.
[17] Cao, Y., Wang, Y., Zhao, X., Zhu, M., & Xu, Z. (2018). Cover block decoupling for content-adaptive H.264 steganography. *IH MMSec 2018 – Proceedings 6th ACM Workshop on Information Hiding and Multimedia Security* (pp.23–30).
[18] Razafindradina, H. B., & Karim, A. M. (2013). Blind and robust images watermarking based on wavelet and edge insertion. *International Journal of Cryptography and Information Security*, *3*(3), 23–30.
[19] Deepikaa, S., & Saravanan, R. (2019). VoIP steganography methods, a survey. *Cybernetics and Information Technology*, *19*(1), 73–87.

[20] Nithyanandam, P., Ravichandran, T., Priyadharshini, E., & Santron, N. M. (2012). An image steganography for color images using lossless compression technique. *International Journal of Computer Science and Engineering*, 7(3), 194–205.

[21] Horé, A., & Ziou, D. (2010). Image quality metrics: PSNR vs. SSIM. In *Proceedings of the International Conference on Pattern Recognition*, 2366–2369. https://doi.org/10.1109/ICPR.2010.579

[22] Sara, U., Akter, M., & Uddin, M. S. (2019). Image quality assessment through FSIM, SSIM, MSE and PSNR—a comparative study. *Journal of Computer Communication*, 7(3), 8–18.

[23] Alexan, W., El Beheiry, M., & Gamal-Eldin, O. (2020). A comparative study among different mathematical sequences in 3D image steganography. *International Journal of Computing and Digital Systems*, *90*(4), 545–552.

[24] Banik, B. G., & Banik, A. (2020). Robust, imperceptible and blind video steganography using RGB secret, maximum likelihood estimation and Fibonacci encryption. *International Journal of Electronic Security and Digital Forensics*, *12*(2), 174–199.

[25] Pilania, U., Tanwar, R., Zamani, M., & Manaf, A. A. (2022). Framework for video steganography using integer wavelet transform and JPEG compression. *Future Internet*, *14*(9), 1–16.

[26] Kumar, P., & Singh, K. (2018). An improved data-hiding approach using skin-tone detection for video steganography. *Multimedia Tools and Applications*, *77*(18), 24247–24268.

[27] Parah, S. A., Sheikh, J. A., Loan, N. A., & Bhat, G. M. (2017). A robust and computationally efficient digital watermarking technique using inter block pixel differencing. *Intelligence Systems Reference Library*, *115*, 223–252.

[28] Banerjee, A., & Jana, B. (2019). A robust reversible data hiding scheme for color image using Reed–Solomon code. *Multimedia Tools and Applications*, https://doi.org/10.1007/s11042-019-7626-0

11
A Substitution-Based Reliable and Stable Video Steganography to Hide Multimedia Files

11.1 Introduction

Embedding secret information is not new; it has been used in different forms for over 1,000 years. Physical steganography means the use of a physical medium to carry secret information. In ancient Greece, the king selected messengers to conceal secret data and save their heads [1]. The secret message is then written on the head of the messenger. After writing the message, the hair could return to hide the secret message. When the hair is long on the head of the messenger, he is sent to deliver the message. For reading, the recipient shaves the head of the messenger and reads the message. Then, ordinary objects were used to embed secret messages during the Second World War. Invisible ink was used to hide information on paper so that the paper appears just as an absolute blank to a third party [2]. To retrieve secret information, liquids such as vinegar, fruit juices, and milk were applied since when each one of these substances is heated, they become dim and become observable to human eyes. Nowadays, users use digital steganography to hide secret messages in multimedia cover files. Steganography hides the presence of a secret communication from a third party [3].

Table 11.1 represents a comparison of encryption and embedding techniques. Encryption techniques can be combined with steganography and watermarking. With a combination of encryption and embedding techniques, security can be improved, but at the same time, complexity increases. The validity of steganography techniques

DOI: 10.1201/9781003504139-11

Table 11.1 Comparison of Security Systems

PARAMETERS	CRYPTOGRAPHY	WATERMARKING	STEGANOGRAPHY
Objective	Secret writing	Verify identity and authenticity	Hide secret information
Goal	Protect data	Trace source, copyright protection, and Fraud detection	Store and forward secret information
Visibility	Always visible	Sometime visible	Never
Challenges	Key management	Robustness	Imperceptibility, payload, robustness

can be measured by concealing capacity, imperceptibility, and complexity [4]. Capacity is the quantity of confidential information that could be embedded inside a cover [5]. Imperceptibility is the visual excellence of the stego [6]. Complexity is the time spent concealing and extracting confidential messages [7]. For imperceptibility check, PSNR, MSE, histogram analysis, and entropy are calculated [8]. The complexity of the proposed work is measured in seconds.

11.2 Literature Review and Gaps

Whenever users try to achieve any one parameter, such as concealing capacity, imperceptibility, or complexity, then that can be obtained easily, and it is also evident from the literature review. Problems arise when the user wants to achieve these parameters in combination. When the user tries to improve the embedding capacity, he needs to compromise with the other two parameters: complexity and imperceptibility. When many secret messages are embedded, distortion will be introduced in the cover file, resulting in poor visual quality for the stego. The poor visual quality of stego will lead to exposure of embedded secret information, resulting in low robustness.

The video was taken as the cover for the research work [13]. The LSB was applied to embed the confidential message inside the video cover. A secret message was reserved in the form of a surreptitious image. The video frames were extracted and chosen based on the 5D hyper-chaotic method to embed the secret information as an image. The hidden information was also decomposed into several blocks, which were embedded into frames chosen by the 5D chaotic method. The proposed work was analyzed based on PSNR, MSE, Concealing Capacity, Correlation Coefficient (CC), etc. From the experimental results, it was determined that the work was reliable and stable for real-life applications. The authors proposed another substitution technique, PVD, in [14].

The proposed research work addressed two challenges: the Falling-Off Boundary Problem (FOBP) or the Incorrect Extraction Problem (IEP). The cover image was decomposed into 2 × 2-pixel blocks for hiding secret information. Secret-information hiding was done by exploring horizontal, vertical, and diagonal directions for every block. For each block, the difference value of pixels was calculated in all directions. Then, secret information was embedded by taking the difference value and the remainder of pixel pairs. Different attacks have been applied to the stego file to detect the confidential message, but the method was robust enough to retain the hidden data. PSNR, MSE, CC, and FOBP values were also calculated for work security analysis.

Steganography is the way to hide secret data so that no one knows its existence except the sender. In paper [15], image steganography was proposed by the authors using the CNNs technique. The authors named the proposed technique SteGuz. It used a CNN three times to complete the concealing and retrieving of secret data. It introduced a new function, the gain function, depending on the SSIM value. For validation of the experimental results, the authors embedded different secret images. It has been determined that the proposed research work was robust and highly imperceptible.

Scholars have done much work in steganography, but many challenges still exist. To overcome some of the difficulties, authors proposed a hybrid substitution technique in the paper [16]. They first performed encryption and then embedded the secret data using a combination of LSB and MSB. The proposed technique conceals secret information randomly in the cover file, resulting in more security and robustness. The work was assessed based on the assessment metrics PSNR and MSE. From the simulation, it has been determined that the work performed well compared with the existing substitution techniques.

Although researchers and academicians have been working on the security parameters for several years, many gaps and challenges still exist in the security system during the online transmission of personal information. We designed and developed a video-steganography technique to overcome these gaps and substitute pixels for hiding secret information. The first suitable region of interest is calculated using OpenCV. By embedding personal secret data in the appropriate area of interest, the imperceptibility of the stego file can be improved. Embedding of hidden information is done in the first eight bits. The value of the cover file is changed to odd if one comes, and it is changed to even if zero comes in the cover frame.

11.2.1 Motivation

The proposed research work contributes to overcoming the following gaps:

- The video-steganography technique provides the proper balance between embedding capacity, imperceptibility, and complexity.
- Through appropriate steps of optimization, computational overhead is balanced.
- A new hybrid technique that satisfies all parameters of online communication.
- The proposed technique can efficiently hide the secret messages of text, PDF, image, audio, and video.

11.3 Proposed Work

OpenCV was launched in 1999 to detect frames from images and videos. It has many versions and can detect frames in different conditions. It is user-friendly and has a simple user interface. It has a strong library and detects frames based on predefined classes. It can detect frames in 3D videos as well. It handles image transformation, scaling, image filtering, color-space conversion, etc. It is open-source and developed by Intel [9]. It has applications in artificial intelligence, machine learning, computer vision, robotics, image processing, etc. It uses different programming languages such as Java, C++, MATLAB, Python, etc. It mainly works on image capturing, image processing, object detection, and object recognition. It represents images into patterns and then performs mathematical operations on these patterns [10]. Its library has more than 2,500 optimized algorithms. It can run on Windows, Mac, Linux, and Android. It has some prerequisites such as Python, NumPy, SciPy, Pandas, Matplotlib, Matrix mathematics, and Vectors [11].

Figures 11.1 and 11.2 represent the complete secret message concealing and extraction process. Video cover files are decomposed into frames using OpenCV. The secret message is taken in different forms such as text, PDF, image, audio, and video. The secret message must be processed before embedding it into the cover file. It is converted to binary form first and then concealed in cover frames using the substitution technique. The encoding and decoding of secret data are shown in Figure 11.4 in detail. When the stego frames combine to generate the stego video, they conceal a secret message. The reverse process is applied at the receiver end to extract a secret message. The retrieved secret information carries good visual quality, nearly equivalent to the original secret information.

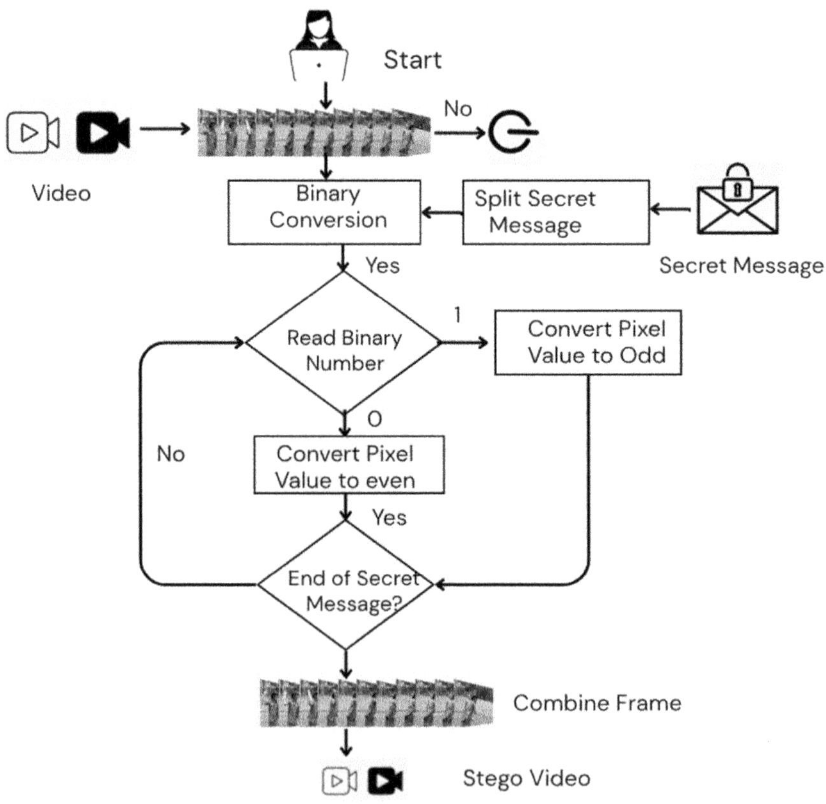

Figure 11.1 Multimedia secret message embedding flowchart.

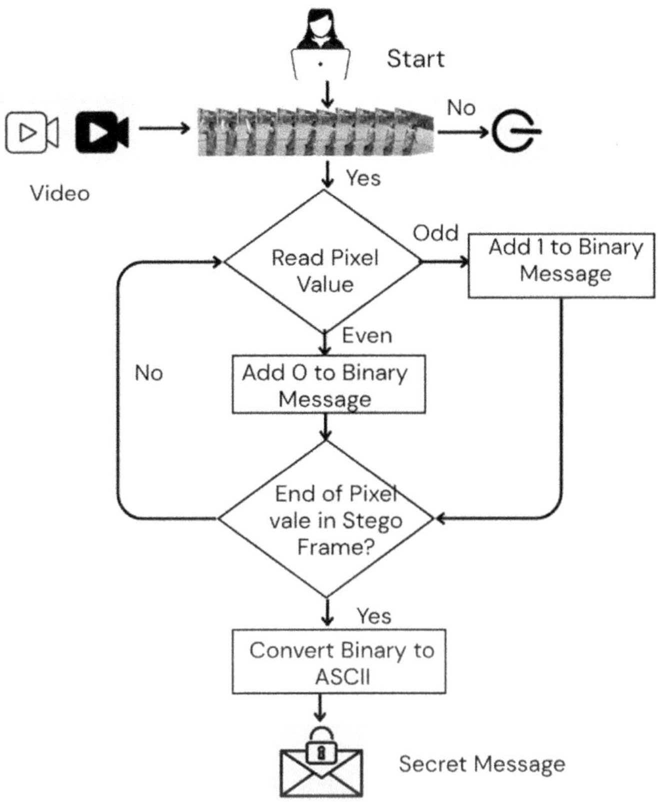

Figure 11.2 Multimedia secret message extraction flowchart.

The process of multimedia-message encoding and decoding is shown in Figure 11.3. The secret message is transformed using its ASCII values into 8-bit binary code. The generated pixels are read from left to right in multiples of three, totaling 9 bits. Eight-bit words are used to store binary information. The value of the cover file is changed to odd if one comes, and it is changed to even if zero comes in the cover frame. Consider whether "Hii" is to be embedded in the cover file. As the secret message carrier has 3 bytes, the total number of pixels needed to hide the message is 3 x 3 = 9. Thus, to hide 3 x 3 data, a cover of size 4 x 3 is enough. "H" has ASCII value 72, which in binary form equals 01001000.

The first three pixels (27, 64, 164), (248, 244, 194), and (174, 246, 250) are taken to hide the message. The pixels are changed to odd for one and even for 0. After modification, pixels are (26, 63, 164), (248, 243, 194), and (174, 246, 250). The process is repeated until the

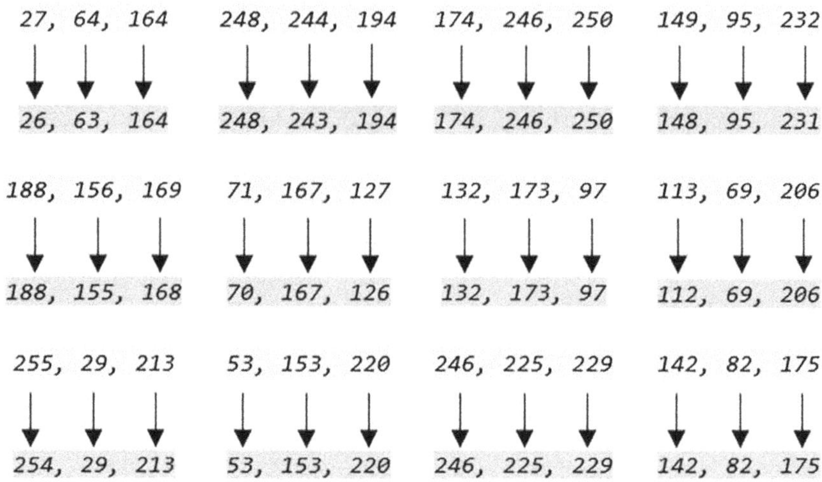

Figure 11.3 Encoding and decoding of secret data.

complete secret message is embedded. Three pixels are taken once to extract a hidden message, until the last value is odd, which means the secret information is extracted completely. Every three-pixel contains binary information, which the same encoding logic can retrieve. If the obtained bits are odd, the binary bit is 1; else, it is set to 0.

11.3.1 Algorithm for Multimedia-Message Encoding

The algorithm is used to extract frames from the input video. The first step in removing the frame is to check if the *tmp* directory has been created. If the *tmp* directory is not created, we create a new tmp directory. With the OS library, we can read or create new directories. The input video is captured and stored in the vidcap variable. Frames are extracted using OpenCV. The process of frame extraction repeats itself until the loop is true. Video is read, and capture frames are stored in the variable "image" until valid. When the condition is not met, reading the frame is stopped. Finally, it is stored in the "tmp" directory. Maths and the Numpy library perform all the mathematical functions. These extracted frames are now used to embed the secret message. The frames are selected randomly for embedding secret messages because randomness improves security.

Input: Video, Secret_Message
Output: Extracted Frames, Stego_Video
Start
1 vidcap← copy (Video);// Copy input video in vidcap
2 while (True)
2.1 [frm, n] ←extract_frames using OpenCV(vidcap)
2.2 else terminate loop
3 A random number is selected, and based on that number, the secret message is decomposed using math. ceil function
3.1 initialize per_c ← math.ceil(len(s_str)/ random(range(len(s_str))));
3.2 str ← "", split_list ← [], cnt←0; // Split the secret message and store it in str
4 Using the built-in function to convert the secret message into binary before embedding and storing it in an array
4.1 datalist[]←convert_binary(split_list)
4.2 for x in datalist // Embed binary secret message in a frame
4.2.1 if (x=="0" and imdata[count]%2==1)
4.2.1.1 imdata[count] -= 1;
4.2.2 else if (x=="1" and imdata[count]%2==0)
4.2.2.1 imdata[count] += 1;
4.2.3 count +=1;
4.4 Save the modified array as Stego_video
5 Stego_Video ← moviepy.imdata; // Stego video is created using the moviepy function
6 return (Stego_Video)
End

Frames are retrieved from the input video file at 24 frames per second. Randomly, a number is selected, and based on that value, a secret message is decoded. For example, if the randomly selected number is 21, the secret message will be decomposed into 21 parts. The math.*ceil* library will decide how many parts the message can be split into. This algorithm splits the secret message into multiple parts and stores them randomly in several frames. The decomposed parts of the secret message are converted into binary values, and then an array of binary values is created to store the complete secret message. Frames are also decomposed into pixel values, creating an array of pixels for a frame. For embedding purposes, the binary value of the secret message is checked to determine whether it is '1' or '0'. If it is '1', then convert the frame's pixel to odd; otherwise, if the secret bit is '0', then convert the frame's pixel to even.

This way, the complete secret message is embedded into *n* frames. With the updated even and odd values of pixels, new arrays are created for the stego frames. These stego frames are combined to form the stego video. The MoviePy library is used to make a video from frames for a considerable time. The secret message is hidden in more than one frame for security purposes. In an array named "Image_file", all the paths of the generated frames are stored. The retrieved video is finally named "my_video.mp4". Shutil removes or deletes all the unnecessary files.

11.3.2 Algorithm for Multimedia-Message Decoding

Input: Stego_Video,
Output: Secret_Message, Video

Start

1 vidcap ← copy (Stego_Video) extract stego frame from stego video using OpenCV
2 Initialize count ← 0; //Create an empty int variable
3 Repeat it for all stego frames
  3.1 img[] ←vidcap.read() //Read one frame pixel value and store it in an array
  3.2 for y in imdata //Repeat it for every pixel value in the array
    3.2.1 Check if the pixel value is odd or even
    3.2.1.1 if(y%2==0) : Secret_Message += "0" //If it is odd append 1 to variable
    3.2.1.2 else Secret_Message += "1" //If it is even appended 0 to variable
4 Convert a variable value from binary to message using the covert_binary_to_text() built-in function
5 return (Secret_Message)

End

Take input as a stego video and then extract the frames into an empty variable. All the extracted frames are converted into pixel values, creating an array. If the pixel value stored in the array is odd, then for the extraction of the secret message, we append '1' to the value of the variable. Otherwise, if the pixel value is even, then '0' is appended to the variable. The process is repeated for the complete array. Then the updated values of the array are used to create the secret message. Now, the receiver checks the quality of the extracted secret message.

11.4 Performance Evaluation Parameters

The excellence of the work is measured in terms of PSNR, MSE, entropy, and histogram [12]. These parameters work on the statistical properties of the input and output files. The difference between the original and stego file is calculated using the parameters mentioned above. Then, the difference between the two files is used to expose secret messages or check the quality of work. The carrier file is taken as a video for the work, but secret information is taken in different multimedia files. All the evaluation parameters are explained one by one as follows:

11.4.1 PSNR

It is the error existing between the original and the stego image. The higher value of PSNR means that the error between the original and stego image is low. A PSNR value above 40 dB signifies the excellence of the stego file. Equation 11.1 is used to calculate the PSNR value for the research work [13]. MAX_I represents the maximum power of the original signal, and MSE is the error present in the stego file.

$$PSNR = 10\log_{10}\left(\frac{MAX_I^2}{MSE}\right) \tag{11.1}$$

11.4.2 MSE

It is the most extensively used technique in image processing to check the quality of images. It is the squared difference between the original and stego image. The larger the alteration, the higher the error between the original and stego files. Equation 11.2 is used to calculate the MSE for the proposed work [14]. I(i) is the original signal, and J(i) is the stego signal.

$$MSE = \frac{1}{n}\sum_{i=0}^{i=n}\left[I(i) - J(i)\right]^2 \tag{11.2}$$

11.4.3 *Histogram*

Subjective and objective methods can measure the quality of digital images. Subjective methods are based on human perceptual view, but image quality is calculated through a computational technique in objective methods. A histogram represents the digital image in terms of brightness. It is used to describe the pixels in graphical form. Equation 11.3 is used to draw the histogram for the work [15]. His(c) represents the histogram of the original cover file, and His(s) represents the histogram for the stego file.

$$HA = \frac{\sum_{i=1}^{n}\left(His(c) - His(s)\right)^2}{\sum_{i=1}^{n} His(c)^2} \tag{11.3}$$

11.4.4 *Entropy*

It is the measure of uncertainty in the original and stego images. It defines the brightness level that individual pixels can have. The entropy of the input image is calculated using Equation 11.4 for any pixel location, such as image (i, j), where i represents the pixel's location at the X-axis and j represents the pixel's location at the Y-axis [16]. Where N levels and pk is the possibility for level k, with an even probability distribution, entropy can be achieved at its highest. In other words, if $N = 2^n$, then p_k is constant, $p_k = 1/N = 2^{-n}$.

$$E = \sum_{0}^{N-1} p_k log_2\left(p_k\right) \tag{11.4}$$

11.5 Implementation and Result Discussion

The implementation is done in Python using a set of libraries, as Python is user-friendly and has a strong library [17]. The video is occupied as a carrier because of its size and dynamic nature. It improves the concealing capacity of the technique as multiple options are available in the video to hide the confidential information [18]. The confidential message is taken in text, PDF, images, audio, and video, one by one. All the audio and video files are converted to an image first. Then it is converted into binary form before hiding. The cover video is converted into frames using OpenCV, and then frames are chosen randomly to hide the secret message.

Figure 11.4 compares the excellence of the cover and stego frames. Both frames are similar in appearance. The lower difference between the quality of two frames, the lower the chances of detecting a secret message. For validation and verification of the proposed technique, we have taken secret information in different forms, which are text, PDF, image, audio, and video. For checking imperceptibility, PSNR, MSE, Entropy, and Histogram analysis of both images are calculated, which are shown in Table 11.2. We also computed concealing time and retrieval time for secret messages.

The proposed technique works well for all types of secret messages in multimedia. The analysis of the work is shown in Table 11.2. We

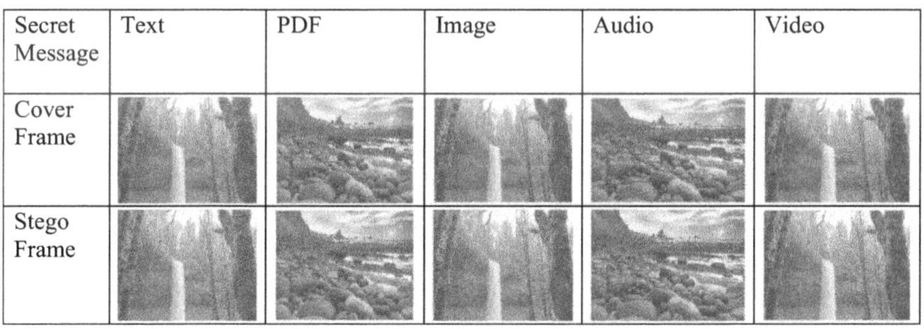

Figure 11.4 Cover and stego frames generation for multimedia secret messages.

Table 11.2 Analysis of Proposed Work

SECRET MESSAGE	TEXT	PDF	IMAGE	AUDIO	VIDEO
Cover Frame Size	12.6MB	64 MB	12.6MB	64.1MB	12.6MB
Secret Message Size	8KB	44KB	4KB	7KB	4KB
PSNR in dB	77.68	62.36	73.34	51.59	71.34
MSE in dB^2	0.0011	0.0377	0.0030	0.4499	0.0030
Entropy of Cover Frame	7.6465	7.7709	7.6465	7.7709	7.7675
Entropy of Stego Frame	7.6467	7.7696	7.6471	7.6750	7.6471
Concealing Time in Seconds	2.82	21.38	3.55	92.20	3.6
Retrieval Time in Seconds	0.23	2.74	0.28	29.9	0.29

have concealed secret messages of different sizes and types every time. The lowest PSNR value calculated is 51.59 dB for an audio secret message, representing the decent visual excellence of the stego file. For text secret messages, PSNR is found to be the highest, at 77.68 dB. MSE is calculated to be 0.001 dB^2 for text secret messages, the least value among secret messages of different types. The highest error present is estimated to be 0.4499 dB^2 for the audio type of secret message.

Entropy for the unique cover frame and stego frame is also calculated and found to be almost the same. Nearly the same entropy value for the original and stego files means a lesser or no chance of detecting the secret message. The concealing and retrieval time is calculated as maximum for the audio secret message, which is 122.1 seconds. The total time taken for text secret messages is 3.05 seconds, the least time among all types of secret messages. Table 11.2 shows that PDF and audio types of secret messages are difficult to conceal in the cover file compared to all other types of secret messages.

Table 11.3 shows histograms of original and stego frames for all the multimedia secret messages. The histogram represents all three color components, which are red, green, and blue. The X-axis signifies the frequency of pixels, and the Y-axis indicates the number of pixels in the image or frame. The lower the difference between two images or frames, the less the chances of detecting a secret message from the stego file.

11.5.1 Quantitative Analysis

A comparison of work is done with papers [17, 18, 19, 20]. The work is compared based on PSNR and MSE values. Figure 11.5 compares MSE values for embedding secret messages inside the video cover file. We have taken the image as the hidden message for the comparison. For the proposed work, the MSE value is very low, equal to 0.003 dB^2 for an image secret message. However, two existing papers in the comparison have a low value of MSE compared with the proposed work. The value of the error present will change with the variation in the size of the confidential message and the cover. When the amount of the secret message we want to hide increases, the percentage of errors also increases. The low value of MSE means negligible or no error present in the stego file.

Table 11.3 Histograms for Original and Stego Frames

<table>
<tr><th>SECRET MESSAGE</th><th>HISTOGRAM OF ORIGINAL COVER FRAME</th><th>HISTOGRAM OF STEGO FRAME</th></tr>
<tr><td>Text</td><td>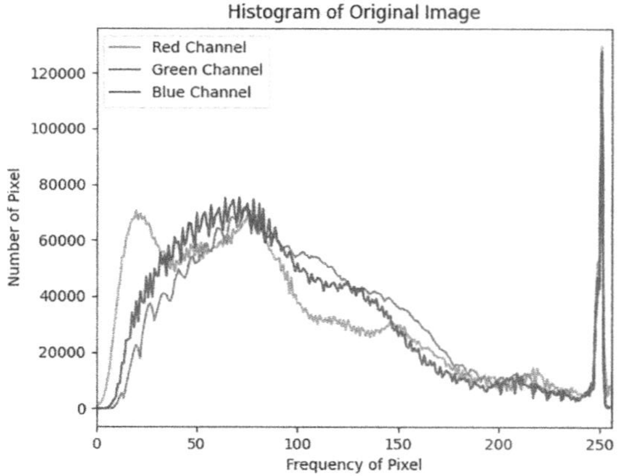
</td><td>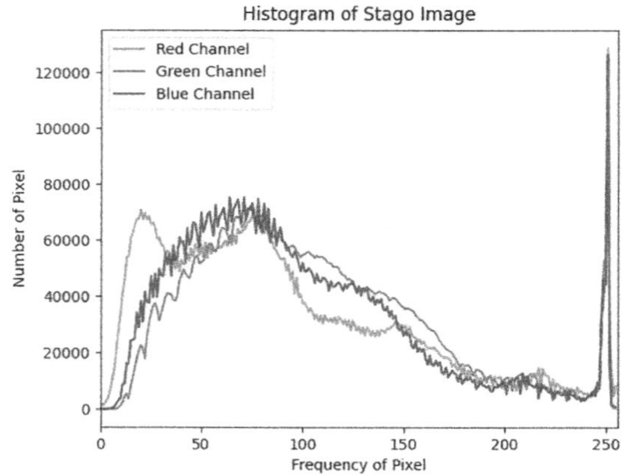
</td></tr>
<tr><td>PDF</td><td>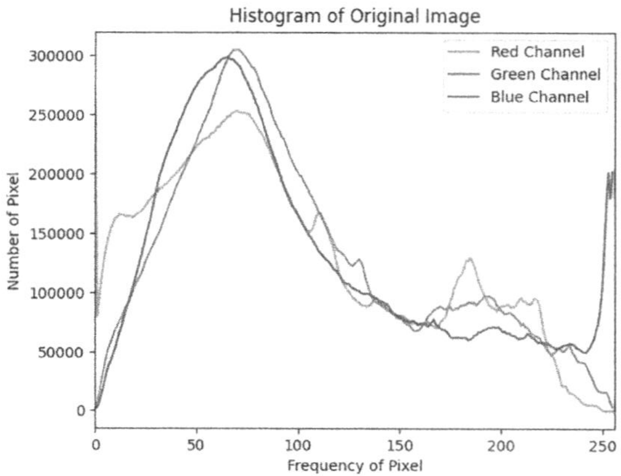
</td><td>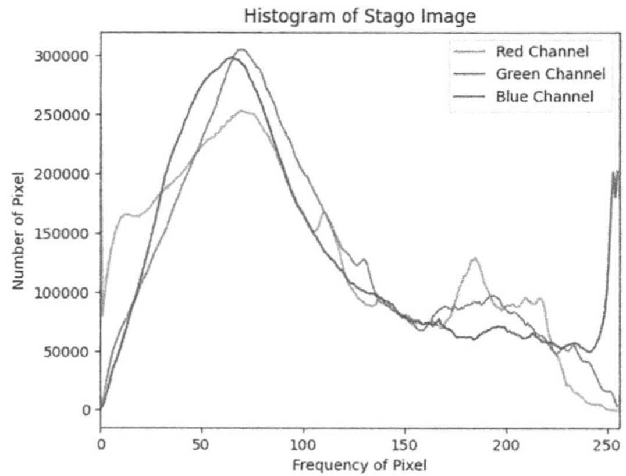
</td></tr>
</table>

(*Continued*)

Table 11.3 (Continued)

SECRET MESSAGE	HISTOGRAM OF ORIGINAL COVER FRAME	HISTOGRAM OF STEGO FRAME
Image	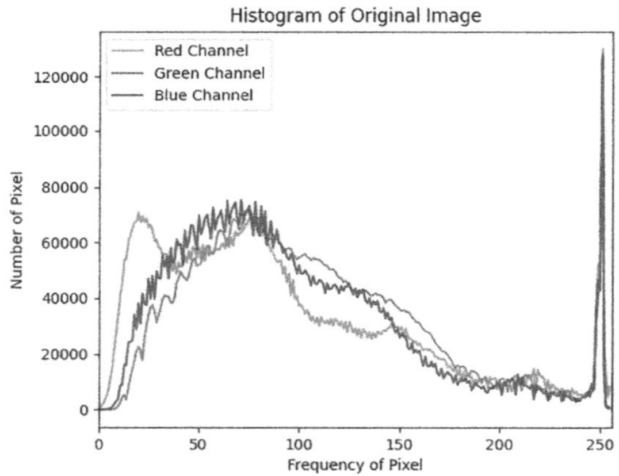	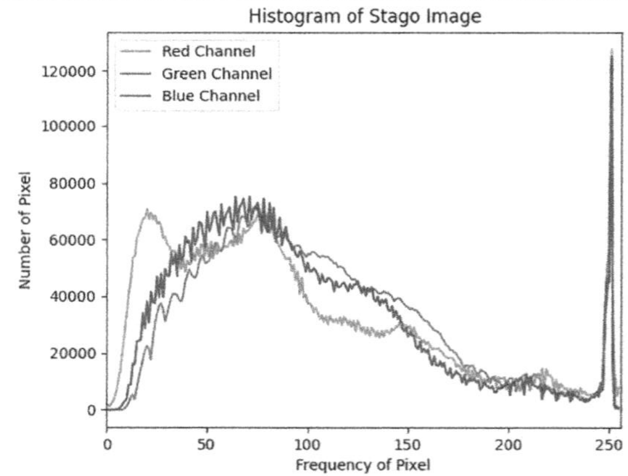
Audio	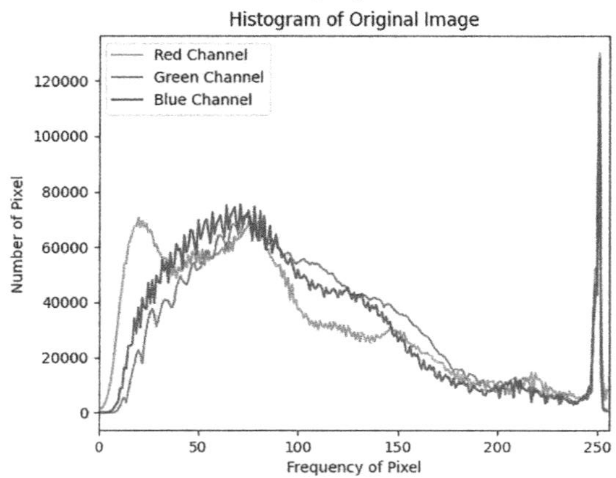	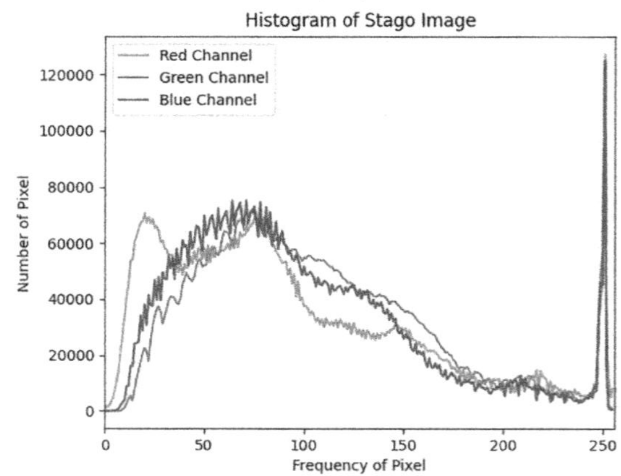

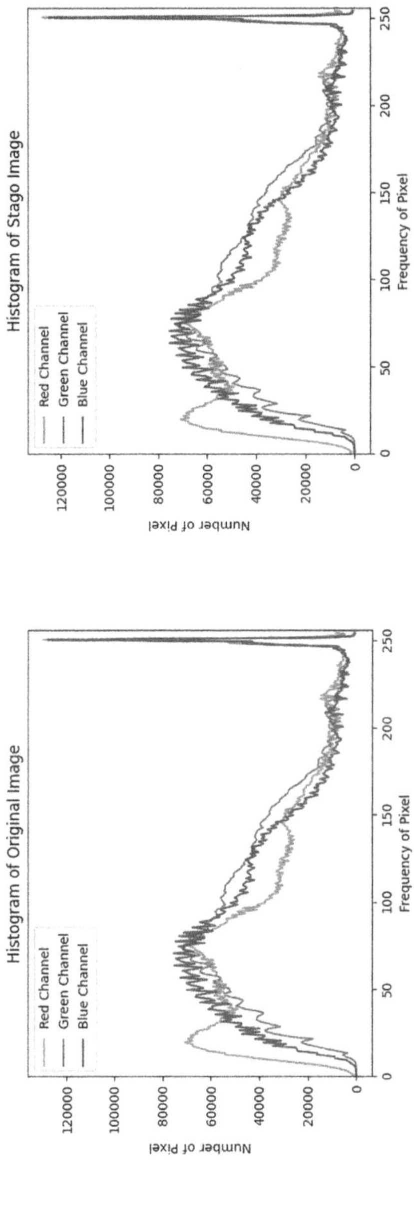
Histogram of Original Image
Red Channel
Green Channel
Blue Channel
Number of Pixel
Frequency of Pixel
Histogram of Stago Image
Red Channel
Green Channel
Blue Channel
Number of Pixel
Frequency of Pixel

Video

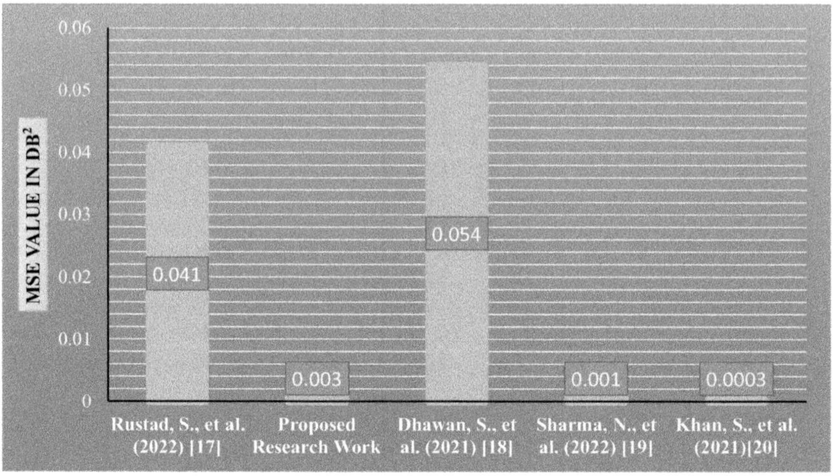

Figure 11.5 Comparison of MSE Value.

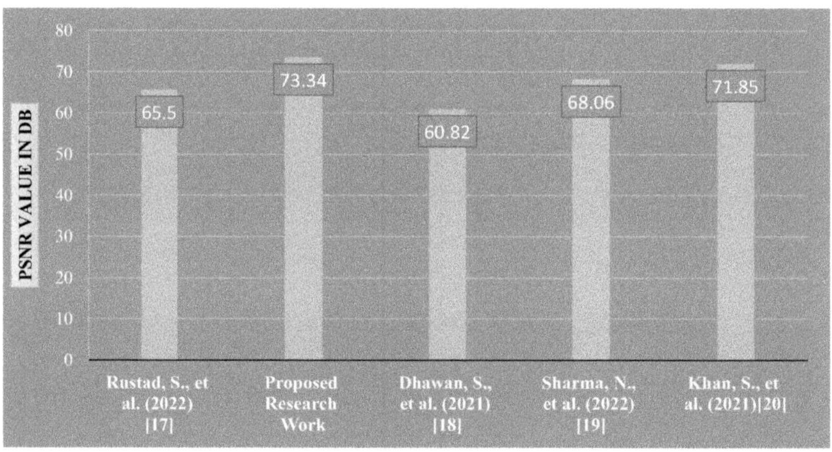

Figure 11.6 Comparison of psnr value.

In Figure 11.6, a comparison of PSNR value is done with papers Rustad, S., et al [17], Dhawan, S., et al. [18], Sharma, N., et al. [19], and Khan, S., et al. [20]. PSNR value measures the imperceptibility of the work. Imperceptibility represents the visual excellence of the stego file. The higher the imperceptibility, the lower the chances of detecting a secret message. For the proposed work, PSNR is approximately equal to 71.34 dB. A PSNR value greater than 35 dB is considered a good value, meaning the stego file carries almost the same visual quality as the original file.

To validate the research, we also worked on other parameters such as Entropy, Histogram analysis, Concealing time, Retrieval time, etc. Concealing and retrieval time is optimized, equal to a few seconds. The total time taken for text, image, and video covers is between 3 and 4 seconds. For PDF, the total time taken to embed and extract the secret message is calculated to be 24 seconds. For the audio cover file, the total time taken in embedding and retrieval is found to be equal to 122 seconds. Entropy is calculated for both the original cover and the stego file. There is a negligible difference between the two files' entropy, representing the work's visual excellence. We worked on all types of multimedia secret files and can hide any multimedia files in video cover files with good results. The proposed technique is suitable for any multimedia file and satisfies all online communication requirements.

11.5.2 Observations

A few observations for the proposed work have been listed as follows:

- The designed technique can efficiently embed any secret message, including text, image, audio, PDF, and video. Table 11.2 represents the analysis of the proposed work in terms of evaluation parameters.
- Encoding and decoding the secret message is done by the proposed substitution method, as shown in Figure 11.3.
- The technique takes a very reasonable time in embedding and extracting the secret message, which is approximately 3 seconds, as shown in Table 11.2.
- It can embed good-sized secret messages without compromising the visual quality of the stego file. The quality of the stego file is the same as that of the original cover file, as shown in Figure 11.4. Table 11.3 of the histogram analysis also represents the visual excellence of the work.
- A comparative analysis of the proposed technique is shown in Figures 11.5 and 11.6. Comparison shows two parameters, MSE and PSNR. With a change in the type of secret message embedded, the value of MSE and PSNR varies; it has been found that the proposed work performed better in terms of

PSNR than the state-of-the-art methods. The MSE values of state-of-the-art techniques, Rustad, S., et al [17], Dhawan, S., and Khan, S., et al. [20], are better than the proposed work.

- As no additional hardware is required to implement the technique, the technique is cost-efficient.
- It has been concluded from Table 11.2 of experimental results that PDF and Audio files are difficult to embed compared to any other files, such as text, images, and video.
- The proposed technique is simple and can secure secret information during real-time transmission.

11.6 Conclusion

The novelty of the work is that we can embed any multimedia secret messages, such as text, PDF, images, audio, and video, in the video cover file. The proposed technique achieved good experimental results compared to the existing work in the same field. PSNR, MSE, Entropy, and Histogram are drawn to check the imperceptibility of the work. The complexity is measured in concealing and retrieval time for the job in a few seconds. A comparison of the proposed work is also done with four existing techniques. We have used evaluation parameters such as PSNR and MSE to compare. It has been concluded that the proposed technique is suitable for hiding any multimedia file for a considerable time. It can be used to transmit the hidden secret message in real-time communication.

We can take cover videos of different formats to embed multimedia secret information in the future. We can check the compatibility of other video formats for real-time transmission of embedded secret information.

References

[1] Cao, H., Hu, F., Sun, Y., Chen, S., & Su, Q. (2022). Robust and reversible color image watermarking based on DFT in the spatial domain. *Optik*, 169319.

[2] Sun, H., Qu, Z., Sun, L., Chen, X., & Xu, G. (2022). High-efficiency quantum image steganography protocol based on double-layer matrix coding. *Quantum Information Processing*, 21(5), 1–27.

[3] Subramanian, N., Elharrouss, O., Al-Maadeed, S., & Bouridane, A. (2021). Image steganography: A review of the recent advances. IEEE Access.

[4] ALRikabi, H. T., & Hazim, H. T. (2021). Enhanced Data Security of Communication System Using Combined Encryption and Steganography. *International Journal of Interactive Mobile Technologies,* 15(16).

[5] Alqadi, Z., Sharadqh, A., Asad, N., Shayeb, I., Al-Azzeh, J., & Ayyoub, B. (2019). A highly secure method of secret message encoding. *International Journal of Research in Advanced Engineering and Technology*, 5(3), 82–87.

[6] Hidayasari, N., & Yanto, F. (2020, April). Analysis of the Least Significant Bit Method Using Sequential Encoding-Decoding in Steganography Digital Image. In International Conference on Science and Engineering (Vol. 3, pp. 201–205).

[7] Pilania, U., & Gupta, P. (2019). A Proposed Optimized Steganography Technique using ROI, IWT, and SVD. *International Journal of Information Systems & Management Science, Forthcoming*.

[8] Pilania, U., & Gupta, P. (2020). Analysis and implementation of the IWT-SVD scheme for video steganography. In *Micro-Electronics and Telecommunication Engineering* (pp. 153–162). Springer, Singapore.

[9] Pilania, U. (2021). Stable High-Capacity Video Steganography in Wavelet Domain. *Turkish Journal of Computer and Mathematics Education (TURCOMAT)*, *12*(7), 2142–2158.

[10] Anusha, M., Bhanu, K. N., & Divyashree, D. (2020, July). Secured Communication of Text and Audio using Image Steganography. In *2020 International Conference on Electronics and Sustainable Communication Systems (ICESC)* (pp. 284–288). IEEE.

[11] Osman, O. M., Kanona, M. E. A., Hassan, M. K., Elkhair, A. A. E., & Mohamed, K. S. (2022). Hybrid multistage framework for data manipulation by combining cryptography and steganography. *Bulletin of Electrical Engineering and Informatics*, *11*(1), 327–335.

[12] Almazaydeh, W. E. I. A. (2022). Image Steganography to Hide Unlimited Secret Text Size. *International Journal of Computer Science & Network Security*, *22*(4), 73–82.

[13] Shehab, J. N., Abdulkadhim, H. A., & Al-Tameemi, T. F. (2021). Robust large image steganography using LSB algorithm and 5D hyper-chaotic system. *Bulletin of Electrical Engineering and Informatics*, *10*(2), 689–698.

[14] Sahu, A. K., Swain, G., Sahu, M., & Hemalatha, J. (2021). Multi-directional block-based PVD and modulus function image steganography to avoid FOBP and IEP. *Journal of Information Security and Applications*, *58*, 102808.

[15] Khalifa, A., & Guzman, A. (2022). Imperceptible image steganography using symmetry-adapted deep learning techniques. *Symmetry*, *14*(7), 1325.

[16] Iqbal, U. (2021). Hybrid image steganography method with random embedding of encrypted message. *Lahore Garrison University Research Journal of Computer Science and Information Technology*, *5*(4), 36–49.

[17] Rustad, S., Syukur, A., & Andono, P. N. (2022). Inverted LSB image steganography using the adaptive pattern to improve imperceptibility. *Journal of King Saud University-Computer and Information Sciences*, 34(6), 3559–3568.

[18] Dhawan, S., Chakraborty, C., Frnda, J., Gupta, R., Rana, A. K., & Pani, S. K. (2021). SSII: Secured and high-quality steganography using intelligent hybrid optimization algorithms for IoT. *IEEE Access*, 9, 87563–87578.

[19] Sharma, N., Chakraborty, C., & Kumar, R. (2022). Optimized multimedia data through computationally intelligent algorithms. *Multimedia Systems*, 29(5), 2961–2977.

[20] Khan, S., Abbas, N., Nasir, M., Haseeb, K., Saba, T., Rehman, A., & Mehmood, Z. (2021). Steganography-assisted secure localization of smart devices in the internet of multimedia things (IoMT). *Multimedia Tools and Applications*, *80*(11), 17045–17065.

12

Challenges and Future Trends in Steganography

12.1 Introduction

Steganography is an ancient way of hiding information. The word comes from the Greek words covered and written. It has been used for centuries. Today, steganography is in progress and allows you to hide data in digital formats such as images, audio, music, PDF, network, 3D content, and video. Despite this progress, there are still many challenges. Steganalysis techniques need to be designed for the amount of information that can be recognized and hidden without being noticed. Ethical concerns also arise due to the concealed secret data [1].

Many types of steganography techniques are categorized based on the medium used to hide information. Image steganography is one of the most common formats in which data is hidden in image files by changing pixel values. Text steganography is limited to hiding secret messages in textual form and typically supports only small amounts of data. Images are the most common way of information sharing on the web so image steganography is very popular among the researchers. Image steganography can be implemented in both the spatial and transform domain [2]. In it, data are embedded in part of image and it has large embedding capacity compared with text steganography. In audio steganography, secret data is hidden in unwanted noise.

Video steganography is also more popular like image steganography. Video has multiple frames and more than one frame can be used to hide the secret information, which also add randomness, resulting into robustness. It has dynamic nature, so there are fewer chances of the detection of hidden secret messages [3]. These days 3D steganography

DOI: 10.1201/9781003504139-12

is also used to hide the secret data. 3D steganography also has a high concealing capacity as secret data can be hidden in all three dimensions. In network steganography secret data is concealed in traffic, protocol headers, and noise etc. But in network steganography latency, delay and rerouting may cause detection of hidden information [4].

12.2 Challenges in Steganography

Steganography techniques have several challenges when hiding and transmitting secret data. One of the main issues is evidence of when steganography techniques become more demanding. It is a delicate balance to ensure the inhumanity of hidden information without affecting the quality of media files such as images and audio. Another challenge is capacity, as the amount of data that can be hidden without detection is often limited. Furthermore, robustness is a problem. Steganography data can easily be lost or corrupted when compressed, resized, or formatted carrier files. There are also security concerns, as steganography, which is poorly implemented for reverse development operations, is susceptible to being affected. With the increasing number of digital communications tests, whether hidden content is present, even steganography can be determined. Finally, doubts could increase. Some of the challenges are explained and shown through Figure 12.1.

Detection and Countermeasures: Steganalysis has improved and uses machine learning or statistical methods, which threatens the way information is secretly stored. Using intelligence detection tools makes creating hidden information that cannot be found more difficult. Digital forensic experts can recognize abnormalities in digital files that may contain hidden details. As forensic skills grow, those who want to hide data must find a stronger opportunity to do this [5]. The PSNR, Structural Similarity Index Metric (SSIM), and Normalized Cross Correlation (NCC) could be utilized for the detection of hidden information. The larger the value of these metrics, the harder it is to detect the hidden secret information. PSNR compares the quality of the stego file to the original file. The steganography technique is considered robust if

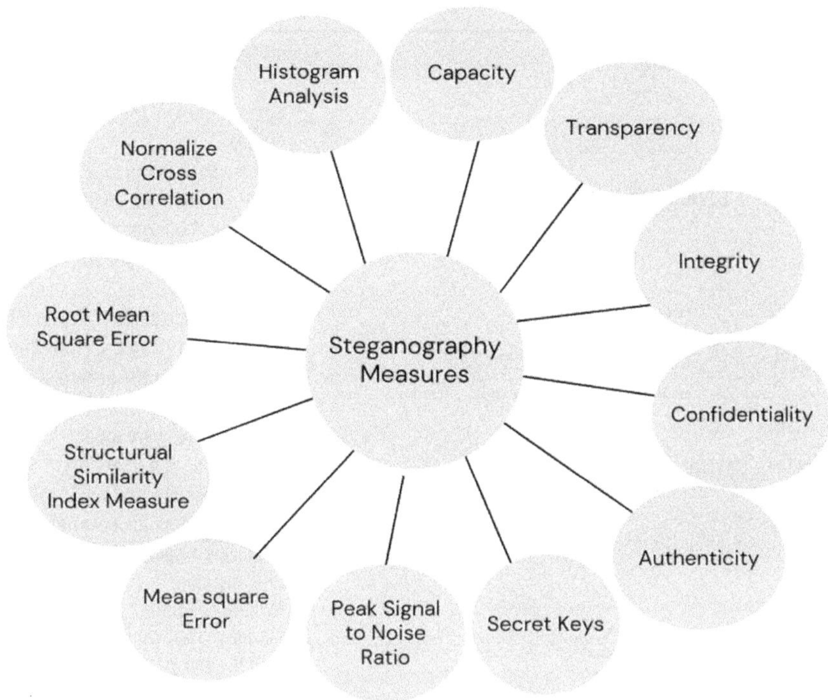

Figure 12.1 Challenges with steganography [4].

the difference between the two is less than a certain threshold. NCC measures how closely the original and stego images are similar. It has a value from 0 to 1. Where 1 represents very few chances of detecting a hidden secret message. SSIM compares the structure of the original and stego images to measure the quality of the steganography technique. It also works on contrast, luminance, and visual perceptions. Table 12.1 shows the mathematical representation of performance metrics.

Capacity and Robustness: When hiding data, you must correct the hidden capacity to keep the original appearance of information. Hiding too much data can make detection easier. Therefore, it is essential to find the right balance. Digital media such as photos and videos are often exposed to compression and size changes. The main challenge for steganographers is ensuring that hidden messages remain intact and none of these

Table 12.1 Performance Metrics

MSE [6]	$MSE = \frac{1}{n}\sum_{i=1}^{n}(y_i - y_i)^2$	(1)	Where n- number of samples, y_i is the actual value of the ith data point, and y_i is the predicted value.
PSNR [7]	$PSNR = 10.\log_{10}\left(\frac{MAX_I^2}{MSE}\right)$	(2)	Where MAX_I is the maximum pixel value of the input image, and the MSE error between the original and the generated stego image
NCC [8]	$NCC = \frac{\sum_{i=1}^{n} x_i \times y_i}{\sqrt{\sum_{i=1}^{n} x_i^2} \times \sqrt{\sum_{i=1}^{n} y_i^2}} \pi r^2$	(3)	Where x_i represents the element in the input image, y_i represents the element in the generated stego image.
SSIM [9]	$SSIM(x,y = \frac{(2\mu_x\mu_y + C_1)(2\sigma_{xy} + C_2)}{(\mu_x^2 + \mu_y^2 + C_1)(\sigma_x^2 + \sigma_y^2 + C_2)}$	(4)	Where x and y are input images, μ_x and μ_y are the intensities of x and y, σ is the variance, σ^2 is the covariance, and C is a constant to stabilize the division.
RMSE [10]	$RMSE = \sqrt{\frac{1}{n}\sum_{i=1}^{n}(y_i - y_i')^2}$	(5)	Where n- number of samples, y_i is the actual value of the ith data point, and yi' is the predicted value.

transformations remain [11]. The Root Mean Square Error (RMSE), Mean Square Error (MSE), Histogram Analysis, and NCC could be utilized to find how robust the steganography technique is. MSE measures the error between the original and the stego file. The lower the error, the fewer the chances of detecting a hidden message. RMSE provides the magnitude of error present and can be used to detect steganography.

Algorithm Complexity and Efficiency: Many enhancement options for hiding sensitive data require a lot of computer performance. It is tough to do such calculations on traditional computers. For algorithm training, computers with a GPU or a TPU are required. Balancing all the parameters like hiding capacity, robustness, and imperceptibility is challenging [12]. When changing any of the mentioned parameters, the others were affected automatically. So, changing steganography parameters results in low transparency, loss of integrity of data, and loss of confidentiality of secret information.

12.3 Future Trends in Steganography

The future of covert messaging holds strong relations to technological progressions, predominantly in. AI, deep learning, and quantum computing. An emerging pattern is utilizing AI-guided concealing techniques, where profound learning designs can independently receive and conceal secret information into multimedia reports in ways that are increasingly difficult to identify. In parallel, changing concealing techniques have been invented to opt for concealing strategies influenced by the substance and circumstance of communication media, improving functionality and protection [13].

Adaptive arrangements study carrier content and context to maximize protection while maintaining high functionality of hidden data [8, 9]. Cutting edge brings new questions on how concealed ciphers adapted to each specific communication could balance detectability and large capacity throughput. Quantum computing harnesses quantum properties to safeguard information in novel ways. By leveraging the principles of steganography, data can be concealed within overlapping possibilities. As virtual worlds expand in scope and immersion, fresh avenues for concealing data arise alongside new complications [10]. Figure 12.2 is designed to represent various future trends in steganography techniques.

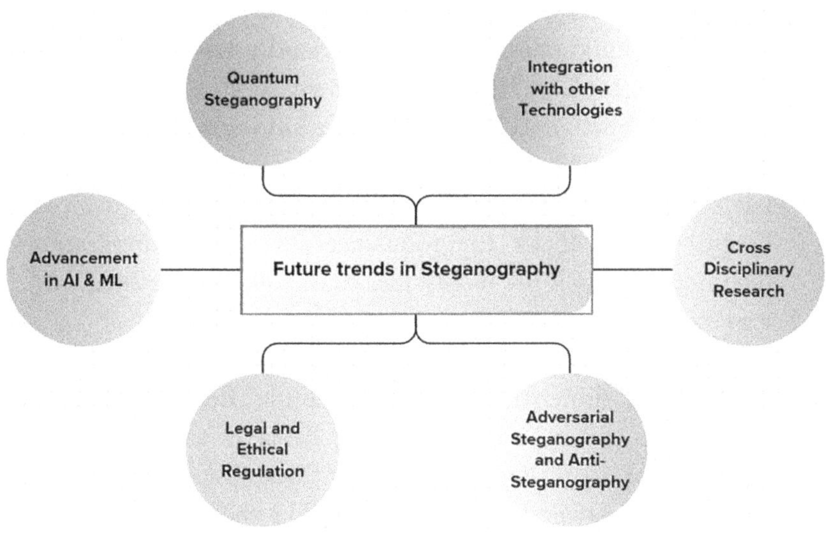

Figure 12.2 Future trends in steganography.

Quantum Computing: These days' quantum computers are in research and lots of work is in progress for the development of these computers. Steganography can be done on quantum computers which require the detailed knowledge of quantum computing. In it secret data can be embedded in different states and it is not easy to detect by the third person [14].

Integration with other Technologies: Steganography using blockchain technology makes your data safe and reliable. This creates a dataset of secret messages that cannot be modified. When IoT devices become increasingly common, the demand for steganography increases to develop and secure all your data. With more people using Augmented Reality (AR) and Virtual Reality (VR), there are new opportunities and challenges to hide information. You need the chance to hide data in a complex multi-layer digital environment. As digital communications increase the wide range of multimedia and interactive formats, there are increasingly unique ways to hide information specially developed for these types of content [15].

Cross-disciplinary Research: The integration of encryption, computer vision, signal processing, and data science experts can create new opportunities to hide and recognize information. To use steganography tools, it is essential to understand how people interact and notice hidden messages. This knowledge helps build effective and user-friendly systems [16].

Anti-steganography: It is also known as the steganalysis techniques which are used to detect the hidden secret messages. Many steganalysis tools and techniques exist but each one has some issues associated with them. These techniques can be utilized to check the robustness of the steganography techniques. But all the techniques must follow the ethical and legal consideration [17].

3D Steganography: In it secret message can be hidden in any of the three dimensions of the cover file. Because of three dimensions it has more concealing capacity than the two-dimensional cover file. But in case of three-dimensional cover file detailed knowledge of it is required by the user [18].

Network Steganography: These days network steganography is gaining attention of researchers. Data are embedded in the network traffic, protocol header, layers of network, and noise [19]. However, in it steganography can be detected is case of delay, latency, rerouting, and retransmission of data. On embedding large size secret data the visual quality of stego may degrade and can cause exposure of hidden information. The balance between embedding capacity, robustness and visual quality of stego is very important as on changing any one of the parameter other two got affected.

Legal and ethical considerations: Legal and ethical consideration is very important to consider before any technique can be applied. Steganography is used to hide the secret data, but it should be used for positive reason only. It should not be used by the people with wrong intension for the misuse of the data. The steganography techniques must be able to balance the individual rights and legal compliances [20].

Steganography in IoT: IoT devices are utilized to hide the secret information in this type of steganography. Low storage memory and processing power is the main issue in these devices. The communication channel can also be utilized to conceal the secret data. These devices have low concealing capacity so on hide large amount of secret data it can be detected by the hackers. The latency, delay, retransmission can cause detection of hidden messages in IoT steganography. Because of low concealing capacity and less robustness against attacks it does not have more of its application in steganography [9].

12.4 Conclusion

Steganography plays an important role in ensuring the safety of secret information. In this chapter authors provided an overview of many steganography techniques such as text, image, audio, video, 3D, network, and quantum computing etc. Authors tried to find the challenges associated with these techniques. One of the major challenge the trade-off between concealing capacity, robustness against image processing attacks, and visual quality of stego file. The integration of machine-learning techniques, quantum computing, steganography in IoT devices, deep-learning techniques, and blockchain is very challenging. Integration of the mentioned techniques causes the increase in complexity, time and resources but on the other side security of sensitive data will be increased.

References

[1] Johnson, N. F., Duric, Z., & Jajodia, S. (2001). *Information hiding: Steganography and watermarking-attacks and countermeasures*. Springer Science & Business Media.

[2] Fridrich, J. (2009). *Steganography in digital media: Principles, algorithms, and applications*. Cambridge University Press.

[3] Provos, N., & Honeyman, P. (2003). Hide and seek: An introduction to steganography. *IEEE Security & Privacy*, *1*(3), 32–44.

[4] Katzenbeisser, S., & Petitcolas, F. A. P. (Eds.). (2000). *Information hiding techniques for steganography and digital watermarking*. Artech House.

[5] Laishram, D., & Tuithung, T. (2018, May). A survey on digital image steganography: current trends and challenges. In *proceedings of the 3rd International Conference on Internet of Things and Connected Technologies* (pp. 26–27).

[6] Bamanga, M. A., & Babando, A. K. (2024). Recent advances in steganography. In J. Mayer (ed.), *Steganography-The Art of Hiding Information: The Art of Hiding Information* (p. 23). IntechOpen.

[7] Singh, A. K. (2020). Data hiding: current trends, innovation and potential challenges. *ACM Transactions on Multimedia Computing, Communications, and Applications*, *16*(3s), 1–16.

[8] Kumar, R., & Singh, H. (2020). Recent trends in text steganography with experimental study. In B. B. Gupta, G. Perez, D. P. Agrawal and D. Gupta (eds), *Handbook of Computer Networks and Cyber Security: Principles and Paradigms* (pp. 849–872). Springer.

[9] Driss, M., Berriche, L., Atitallah, S. B., & Rekik, S. (2025). *Steganography in IoT: A comprehensive survey on approaches, challenges, and future directions*. IEEE Access.

[10] Naeem, S. (2023). Network security and cryptography challenges and trends on recent technologies. *Journal of Applied and Emerging Sciences*, *13*(1), 1–8.

[11] Subhedar, M. S., & Mankar, V. H. (2014). Current status and key issues in image steganography: A survey. *Computer science review*, *13*, 95–113.

[12] Kumar, V., Sharma, S., Kumar, C., & Sahu, A. K. (2023). Latest trends in deep learning techniques for image steganography. *International Journal of Digital Crime and Forensics*, *15*(1), 1–14.

[13] Alhomoud, A. M. (2021). Image steganography in spatial domain: Current status, techniques, and trends. *Intelligent Automation & Soft Computing*, *27*(1).
[14] Kunhoth, J., Subramanian, N., Al-Maadeed, S., & Bouridane, A. (2023). Video steganography: Recent advances and challenges. *Multimedia Tools and Applications*, *82*(27), 41943–41985.
[15] Majeed, M. A., Sulaiman, R., Shukur, Z., & Hasan, M. K. (2021). A review on text steganography techniques. *Mathematics*, *9*(21), 2829.
[16] Pilania, U., Tanwar, R., Zamani, M., & Manaf, A. A. (2022). Framework for video steganography using integer wavelet transform and JPEG compression. *Future Internet*, *14*(9), 254.
[17] Pilania, U., Tanwar, R., & Nandal, N. (2022). Exploring face detection and recognition in steganography. In U. Pilania, R. Tanwar and N. Nandal (eds), *Unleashing the Art of Digital Forensics* (pp. 181–214).
[18] Pilania, U., & Gupta, P. (2020). Analysis and implementation of IWT-SVD scheme for video steganography. In U. Pilania and P. Gupta (eds), *Micro-Electronics and Telecommunication Engineering: Proceedings of 3rd ICMETE 2019* (pp. 153–162). Springer Singapore.
[19] Pilania, U., & Gupta, P. (2019). A proposed optimized steganography technique using ROI, IWT and SVD. *International Journal of Information Systems & Management Science, Forthcoming*.
[20] Pilania, U., Tanwar, R., Gupta, P., & Choudhury, T. (2021). A roadmap of steganography tools: Conventional to modern. *Spatial Information Research*, *29*(5), 761–774.

Index

For Product Safety Concerns and Information please contact our EU
representative GPSR@taylorandfrancis.com
Taylor & Francis Verlag GmbH, Kaufingerstraße 24, 80331 München, Germany

www.ingramcontent.com/pod-product-compliance
Ingram Content Group UK Ltd.
Pitfield, Milton Keynes, MK11 3LW, UK
UKHW020204200926
475702UK00004B/602

* 9 7 8 1 0 3 2 8 2 1 0 7 8 *